GOD talk

The Radical Side of Love

MONICA WITHERS

Unless otherwise noted, scriptures are quoted from The New King James Version of the Bible.

Scripture quotations are taken from The New King James Version. Copyright © 1982 by Thomas Nelson, Inc. Used by permission. All rights reserved.

Scripture quotations marked (AMP) are taken from the Amplified® Bible, Copyright © 1954, 1958, 1962, 1964, 1965, 1987 by The Lockman Foundation. Used by permission. (www.Lockman.org)

Scripture quotations marked (The Message) are taken from The Message. Copyright © 1993, 1994, 1995, 1996, 2000, 2001, 2002. Used by permission of NavPress Publishing Group.

Scripture quotations marked (NLT) are taken from the Holy Bible, New Living Translation, copyright © 1996, 2004, 2007 by Tyndale House Foundation. Used by permission of Tyndale House Publishers, Inc., Carol Stream, Illinois 60188. All rights reserved.

Scripture quotations marked (KJV) are taken from The King James Version. Copyright © 1979, 1980, 1982, Thomas Nelson Inc.

Scripture quotations marked (NIV) are taken from The Holy Bible: New International Version® NIV ®. Copyright © 1973, 1978, 1984 by International Bible Society. Used by permission of Zondervan Publishing House. All rights reserved.

Scripture quotations marked (GNT) are from the Good News Translation in Today's English Version- Second Edition Copyright © 1992 by American Bible Society. Used by Permission.

ISBN 978-0-9891429-5-3
Published by Mountz Media & Publishing
Tulsa, Oklahoma
918.296.0995
www.mountzmedia.com

DEDICATION

I dedicate *The Radical Side of Love* to Jesus Himself. He has shown me what true radical love really is. He has encouraged me, filled me up and shown me how much He loves me. He is always pushing me beyond my comfort zone, saying, **"Yes! You can!"**

I thank Mark, my amazing husband, whose cup is not just half full, but overflowing with joy, dumb jokes and off-the-chart love. He stands in front of me, beside me and behind me, and he keeps me encouraged and believing in myself even when I feel I have nothing to give.

And I also dedicate this book to Tricia, my sister, who is truly by biggest cheerleader and friend.

Thank you all three!

You See Me

You see me.

You know me.

You love me through and through

You called me.

You chose me and said I am with you.

You see me.

You know me

You've called me by name

You love me in spite of my faults.

you love me any way.

Contents

Where your love walk begins...

INTRODUCTION	8
HOW TO USE THIS BOOK	11
FIRST LOVE	16
CAN I LOVE ON YOU A WHILE?	20
NO LOVE - NO LIFE!	22
PUT A NEW SONG IN YOUR ♡	26
LIFT IT UP	30
BLESSINGS FOLLOW	32
SIT DOWN	34
MORE THAN WORDS CAN SAY	38
DROP IT!	42
U CAN CHOOSE	44
RUN LIKE A RIVER	48
YOU'RE NOT MISSING OUT	52
LOOK UP AND SEE	54

SOAK	58	WHO DO YOU THINK YOU ARE?	124
HOW DEEP IS YOUR LOVE?	62	DRAW YOUR BLADE	128
THE GUIDE ON THE INSIDE	66	TOO BIG TO PLAN	132
LOVE COMES AND GOES	68	IT'S NOT ALWAYS EASY	134
IN AN INSTANT	72	WARRIOR PRAISE	136
EYE OF THE STORM	74	LET ME SHOW YOU OFF!	138
DREAMS DO COME TRUE	78	WHOSE BATTLE IS IT?	140
DO YOU HAVE WHAT IT TAKES?	80	RISE UP	144
ORCHESTRATED TIME	82	OUT OF TOUCH AND NOT ENOUGH	146
PRAISE ON YOUR LIPS	86	NOT ENOUGH, CAN'T FIT	150
TWISTED LOVE	88	THOSE VOICES	152
THERE IS A PERFECT LOVE	92	WHATS YOUR NAME?	156
WHAT MATTERS? WORSHIP!	94	BE PROUD	158
IT'S REALLY COOL, LOOK UP!	98	U WILL SHINE	160
NO MATTER WHAT	100	PUT AWAY THE TOYS	164
SEEK THE FINER THINGS	104	A FATHER TO THE FATHERLESS	166
IT'S MY PART, NOT YOURS	106	DON'T THROW YOUR HANDS IN THE AIR!	170
MY WORD IS RICH	108	ENOUGH ALREADY	174
START PLAYING YOUR PART	112	HE IS COMING	176
WHERE ARE THE MIRACLES?	116	MY LIFE IS NO LONGER MY OWN	178
LIFT	118	THE DOORWAY TO RADICAL LOVE	180
HARDENED SHELL	122	LET'S END THIS WITH A BANG!	182

INTRODUCTION

It's almost impossible to talk about the love of God and really understand its impact because we throw the word love around flippantly like any other word. We say, I love ice cream. I love my cat. I love my dog. So to us it seems that love is here today and gone tomorrow. One day we love someone; then they disappoint us, hurt us or say something we don't like and that love goes right out the door. Marriages end every day because one says they fell out of love with the other. They just don't "feel" love anymore.

Then again, some of us feel unlovable. We believe we don't deserve to be loved. Someone who loved us, hurt us, abandoned us or abused us. Honestly...

Love is something a lot of people avoid.

Love is something we just take for granted.

Yet, God's radical love is the answer.

I was listening to a preacher talk about the love of God the other day. It was impossible for him to really get across how deep God's love is. We can't seem to wrap our heads around the love our infinite Father in heaven has for us.

I know there are few who have grasped it, but the majority of us are trying to understand God's love. Or we're trying to earn it. But we must remember that God loved us from the conception of our birth. He knew us when we were in our mother's womb. He has always wooed us with His love.

God says He loves us with an everlasting love. It's eternal and never ending, no strings attached. He doesn't love us because of what we do or don't do. He loves us because we are His children, and when God sees us, He sees the ultimate sacrifice Jesus offered in our behalf.   He sees the precious blood Jesus shed for you and me, and He's well pleased.

God tells us that He so loved the world He gave His only begotten son for us (John 3:16). God tell us even though we did not love Him at the time, He loved us and sent his son to be a propitiation or sacrifice for our sin (1 John 4:10).

As you read of God's love on the pages that follow, let Him love you. Let the words sink deep down in your heart. Meditate on how much He loves you. And remember, it doesn't matter what you do or don't do in this life, God loves you.

He just does.

Listen with all of your heart to these words and ponder them. Then watch how your life will transform. Your love for others will open. Your wounds will heal. Your fellowship with God will increase and deepen.

My heart's desire is for you to be changed. I desire that you understand like never before that you have access to the Almighty God through Jesus Christ. You can talk with Him about all the deep things inside, and He will listen. He will respond and give you direction for your life, if you only believe, trust and walk it out.

Romans 5:5 says the love of God was poured out or shed abroad in your heart. So let this LOVE illuminate and shine throughout your whole life.

LET'S BE DIFFERENT THAN THE REST OF THE WORLD, MY FRIEND.
LET'S JUST GRAB HOLD AND RECEIVE GOD'S LOVE FOR US.

God chose you.

God handpicked you and said about you, "She is mine."

Now let Him just love you!

Monica

1 Corinthians 13:4-7 (The Message)

So, no matter what I say, what I believe, and what I do, I'm bankrupt without love.

Love never gives up.

Love cares more for others than for self.

Love doesn't want what it doesn't have.

Love doesn't strut,

Doesn't have a swelled head,

Doesn't force itself on others,

Isn't always "me first,"

Doesn't fly off the handle,

Doesn't keep score of the sins of others,

Doesn't revel when others grovel,

Takes pleasure in the flowering of truth,

Puts up with anything,

Trusts God always,

Always looks for the best,

Never looks back,

But keeps going to the end.

HOW TO USE THIS BOOK

This isn't your ordinary book. It includes a mix of devotionals, pictures, activities, blank space and ruled lines so you can finish writing this book.

On these many journal pages, write down your thoughts, your prayers, your hopes, your dreams.

Get the pages dirty and wrinkled and hear the voice of God in a radically, new way.

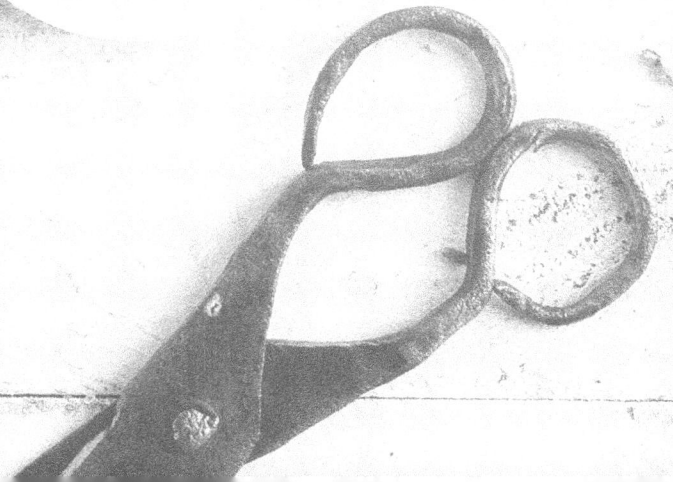

OK. YOUR TURN.

#1. Write out what you think love is.

#2. How would you describe love in your own words?

IT'S NOT ABOUT HOW
MUCH WE LOVE GOD.

IT'S ABOUT HOW
MUCH HE LOVES US!

First Love

When all else fails and you feel overwhelmed, come into MY presence and lay everything down.

Come sit close beside ME and pour out your heart. Don't be afraid to give ME even the things in the dark. Nothing surprises ME, MY dear. But when you shine the light on it, that is when I can tear it out and make things clean again.

Come closely and delight yourself in ME. Come and let ME hold you tight and breathe MY love all over you.

This world can wear you down and make you feel unworthy and dirty all around. But come and be washed by the blood, clean and pure. You are My redeemed, the redeemed of the Lord.

Don't let the distractions pull you away. Let your heart be filled with MY love and MY goodness. Let me say...

I love you. I love you. I love you with all of MY heart. I have given you everything, right from the start. I have said, you are MINE, redeemed, holy and refined. You're made in the image of ME clothed in linen and white.

So be full of cheer and let MY joy overflow. Lift up your face and put a smile there of. MY child, MY dear, you are MY FIRST LOVE!

Redeemed, holy and pure, the daughter, the child of the Most High God!

COLOSSIANS 1:14
IN WHOM WE HAVE REDEMPTION THROUGH HIS BLOOD, THE FORGIVENESS OF SINS.

ISAIAH 43:1
BUT NOW, THUS SAYS THE LORD, WHO CREATED YOU, O JACOB, AND HE WHO FORMED YOU, O ISRAEL:
"FEAR NOT, FOR I HAVE REDEEMED YOU: I HAVE CALLED YOU BY YOUR NAME; YOU ARE MINE."

Seriously, what's it feel like to be God's FIRST LOVE?

_____

_____

Write Him your best love letter!

_____

_____

_____

_____

_____

_____

_____

Now park it, listen and let Him write one to you.

_____

_____

_____

_____

_____

_____

_____

_____

_____

_____

Can I Love On You A While?

Just be still, let ME just love on you awhile. Let me show MYSELF to you.
MY love runs deep. MY love covers all your fears, and all your concerns, and when you
allow MY love to saturate you, then you come to that place of peace, that place I dwell.

So MY beloved, come to that secret place with ME, be still and open your heart and
just receive.

I have much to give you, much for you to see. So come, be still and receive all you can
from ME!

EPHESIANS 2:4 (AMPC)
BUT GOD -- SO RICH IS HE IN HIS MERCY! BECAUSE OF AND IN ORDER TO SATISFY
THE GREAT AND WONDERFUL AND INTENSE LOVE WITH WHICH HE LOVED US.

It's not about how much we love God; it's about how much He loves us, adores us and wants us!

What's stopping you from receiving God's love? If there's something, write it out. How can you just receive?

No Love – No Life!

Why do people resist MY love, child, when love is who I AM?

Love resonates with ME, and with one touch of MY tender hand, a heart can be changed.

The love I have for MY people goes unnoticed, sometimes untouched by fear, a lack of knowledge and rebellion.

Child, let MY love run deep. Let the gates open wide and allow MY love for you to run deeper than ever before. Let it go deeper inside.

Don't hold anything back but only receive. Watch the chains fall away, the hurt subside and the wounds heal up.

MY love is deep, wide and high. And when you truly accept who you are in ME and believe the love God Almighty has for you, then nothing—and I mean nothing—can stop you and the flow of ME.

So let's begin again, today. Open your heart. Open your eyes and receive with open hands...I love you!

Receive it. Expect it. Take it. And then, Walk in it!

1 JOHN 4:16 (AMPC)

AND WE KNOW (UNDERSTAND, RECOGNIZE, ARE CONSCIOUS OF, BY OBSERVATION AND BY EXPERIENCE) AND BELIEVE (ADHERE TO AND PUT FAITH IN AND RELY ON) THE LOVE GOD CHERISHES FOR US. GOD IS LOVE, AND HE WHO DWELLS AND CONTINUES IN LOVE DWELLS AND CONTINUES IN GOD, AND GOD DWELLS AND CONTINUES IN HIM.

EPHESIAN 3:17-19 (NIV)

SO THAT CHRIST MAY DWELL IN YOUR HEARTS THROUGH FAITH. AND I PRAY THAT YOU, BEING ROOTED AND ESTABLISHED IN LOVE, MAY HAVE POWER, TOGETHER WITH ALL THE LORD'S HOLY PEOPLE, TO GRASP HOW WIDE AND LONG AND HIGH AND DEEP IS THE LOVE OF CHRIST, AND TO KNOW THIS LOVE THAT SURPASSES KNOWLEDGE --- THAT YOU MAY BE FILLED TO THE MEASURE OF ALL THE FULLNESS OF GOD.

What does it look like to be truly loved by God? What would the life of a totally loved person look and feel like?

_____

_____

_____

_____

_____

What would your actions look like if you knew and totally believed you are utterly loved and nothing could stop that love?

_____

_____

_____

_____

_____

_____

_____

_____

_____

_____

_____

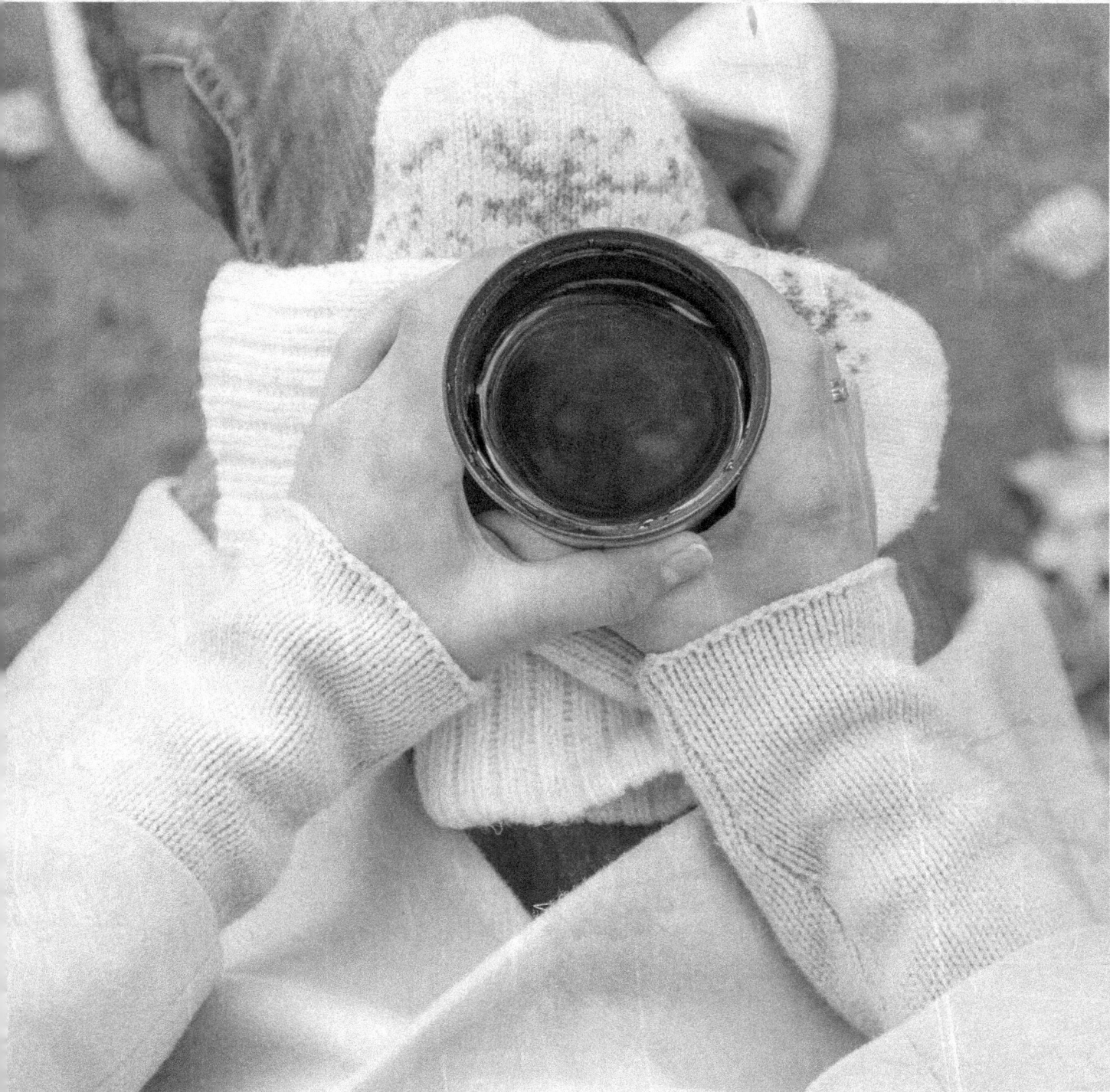

Put a New Song in Your ♥

You fear, you fret when all you need in this moment is to get with ME. Come in to that quiet place. Come directly to ME. Don't hold anything back, but run, run, run really fast!

There are times in this life you will feel lost, overwhelmed and even scared.
Child, listen closely. You have nothing in this world to fear, nothing when you stay close beside ME.

Know MY arms are open wide and you are always safe. You are always able to come and talk quietly with ME.
I want you to know, to truly realize, the love I have for you. You can never compromise.

My love is deep, solid and always full. It never runs dry, and you will never run low.

 So come with ME today. Come to that secret place. Lie yourself down and receive all MY love, mercy and grace. For today is a new day. Yesterday is gone. Press in, and press on.

Put a new song in your heart.
Sing "Jesus Loves Me." Yes, this is true, and Jesus the Savior has handpicked and called you!

PSALM 96:1
OH, SING TO THE LORD A NEW SONG! SING TO THE LORD, ALL THE EARTH.

Here's just the song for you to sing all day long!

Jesus Loves Me

Jesus loves me! This I know,
For the Bible tells me so;
Little ones to Him belong;
They are weak, but He is strong.
Yes, Jesus loves me!
Yes, Jesus loves me!
Yes, Jesus loves me!
The Bible tells me so.

Jesus loves me! This I know,
As He loved so long ago,
Taking children on His knee,
Saying, "Let them come to me!"

Jesus loves me! He who died,
Heaven's gate to open wide;
He will wash away my sin,
Let His little child come in.
Yes, Jesus loves me!
Yes, Jesus loves me!
Yes, Jesus loves me!
The Bible tells me so.

Jesus loves me! loves me still,
When I'm very weak and ill;
From His shining throne on high,
Comes to watch me where I lie.
Yes, Jesus loves me!
Yes, Jesus loves me!
Yes, Jesus loves me!
The Bible tells me so.

Jesus loves me! He will stay,
Close beside me all the way;
He's prepared a home for me,
And some day His face I'll see.
Yes, Jesus loves me!
Yes, Jesus loves me!
Yes, Jesus loves me!
The Bible tells me so.

Poem — Anna Warner 1860
Music — William Bradbury 1862

JOT IT DOWN!

Lift It Up

Lift up your face. Pull your shoulders back and walk forth upright with no lack.

It's a new day, a new time for you. So, child, know you are called, chosen and have been made new.

You are a child of the King, handpicked and called just for ME.
So lift up your head and hold it high, for you are the child of God the Almighty,

God the Most High.

PSALM 3:3
BUT YOU, O LORD, ARE A SHIELD FOR ME,
MY GLORY AND THE ONE WHO LIFTS UP MY HEAD.

1 THESSALONIANS 1:4 (THE MESSAGE)
IT IS CLEAR TO US, FRIENDS, THAT GOD NOT ONLY LOVES YOU VERY MUCH
BUT ALSO HAS PUT HIS HAND ON YOU FOR SOMETHING SPECIAL.

WHEN YOU'VE BEEN HAND-PICKED AND CHOSEN BY SOMEONE SPECIAL OR IMPORTANT, HOW DOES THAT MAKE YOU FEEL OR ACT?

_____

_____

_____

_____

_____

_____

_____

NOW UNDERSTAND!
YOU HAVE BEEN HAND-PICKED AND CHOSEN BY GOD.

Blessings Follow

Sometimes things don't always go according to plans. Sometimes I take you off course to be a blessing to others who otherwise might not see MY handiwork.

I AM looking for those who will lay aside their own agendas, their own plans, to follow the prompting of MY Spirit and who will follow ME wherever I go.

Child, the journey you are on will not always go in the direction and timing of your desire. But know and believe you will always end up exactly where I need you to be.

Blessings follow those who are obedient to ME. Blessings come in many forms and many different ways. But believe the blessings from the Lord are always good and beneficial to you.

MY timing, MY ways are the ways I want you to go. So don't be surprised if your plans for the day fail. Know this is a blessing from heaven, and you will show MY love and MY goodness to a lost soul in need.

So don't be surprised when MY hand moves you beyond your comfort zone — beyond your plans for the day.

Just be full of cheer and excited. Know that you are walking in ME, with ME and for ME in this way.

JEREMIAH 29:11

FOR I KNOW THE THOUGHTS THAT I THINK TOWARD YOU, SAYS THE LORD, THOUGHTS OF PEACE AND NOT OF EVIL, TO GIVE YOU A FUTURE AND A HOPE.

PSALM 119:105 (THE MESSAGE)

BY YOUR WORDS I CAN SEE WHERE I'M GOING; THEY THROW A BEAM OF LIGHT ON MY DARK PATH.

PSALM 25:4-5

SHOW ME YOUR WAYS, O LORD; TEACH ME YOUR PATHS. LEAD ME IN YOUR TRUTH AND TEACH ME, FOR YOU ARE THE GOD OF MY SALVATION;ON YOU I WAIT ALL THE DAY.

You ever been led off course and seen someone's life blessed?

Write it out!

ASK HIM — TAKE ME OFF COURSE, GOD.

Sit Down

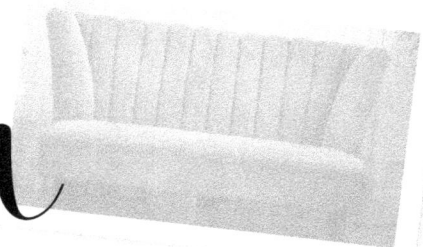

The pressures of life can pull you down and draw you away.

Child, in these times, you need to spend quality time sitting close beside ME listening intently to ME.

The road can get winding and steep, but in MY tight embrace, you will always feel safe and out of harm's way.

So when you feel stressed and out of control—STOP! Sit down where you are. Breathe deeply, breathe slow. Open MY word and listen to ME say: Come all who are weary and burdened. Come close and stay. For MY yoke is easy, and MY burden is light. Be anxious for nothing. Listen and pray.

Stop and rest and hear ME say: You are MY child, the one I adore. Come now and rest your weary soul.

MATHEW 11:28-30 (NIV)
"COME TO ME, ALL YOU WHO ARE WEARY AND BURDENED, AND I WILL GIVE YOU REST. TAKE
MY YOKE UPON YOU AND LEARN FROM ME, FOR I AM GENTLE AND HUMBLE IN HEART, AND YOU WILL
FIND REST FOR YOUR SOULS. FOR MY YOKE IS EASY AND MY BURDEN IS LIGHT."

PHILIPPIANS 4:6 (NIV)
DO NOT BE ANXIOUS ABOUT ANYTHING, BUT IN EVERY SITUATION, BY PRAYER
AND PETITION, WITH THANKSGIVING, PRESENT YOUR REQUESTS TO GOD.

Short list or long list, what are you anxious about? Give it to Him.

_____

_____

_____

_____

Think of scriptures that tell you what God is saying back to you!

_____

_____

_____

_____

_____

STOP WORRYING! BE ANXIOUS FOR NOTHING!

philippians 4:6

WRITE IT OUT!

_____

_____

_____

_____

_____

_____

_____

_____

_____

_____

GRAB IT!
GRAB IT!

More Than Words Can Say

Since the foundation of the world, MY **love** has transformed lives.

I called you in your mother's womb. I chose you before the foundation of this world.

I **love** you. I have **loved** you from the start. No creature, no power, no force can draw you away from MY everlasting **love**.

I have given MY all. I have placed MY **loving** hand upon you and placed MY Spirit on the inside.

My **love** will and is transforming you; MY **love** is leading you down great and mighty paths.

So follow that great **love**, follow MY Spirit, and when you stop and look back, oh what a sight you will see, footprints of you and ME, laid upon the land.

So hear ME say to you this day. My **love**, greater than you can see, but laid down deep in your heart for you only to receive.

Grab it MY dear, grab it with both hands, and when you have hold of it give it away to those all around.

As you receive, it will continue to pour more and more of ME, more and more of MY **love**.

So child listen closely and hear ME today: I **love** you, I **love** you more than words can ever say.

PSALM 139:13-16 (THE MESSAGE)

OH YES, YOU SHAPED ME FIRST INSIDE, THEN OUT; YOU FORMED ME IN MY MOTHER'S WOMB.
I THANK YOU, HIGH GOD YOU'RE BREATHTAKING! BODY AND SOUL, I AM MARVELOUSLY MADE!
I WORSHIP IN ADORATION WHAT A CREATION! YOU KNOW ME INSIDE AND OUT, YOU KNOW EVERY BONE IN MY
BODY; YOU KNOW EXACTLY HOW I WAS MADE, BIT BY BIT, HOW I WAS SCULPTED FROM NOTHING INTO SOMETHING.
LIKE AN OPEN BOOK, YOU WATCHED ME GROW FROM CONCEPTION TO BIRTH; ALL THE STAGES OF MY LIFE WERE
SPREAD OUT BEFORE YOU, THE DAYS OF MY LIFE ALL PREPARED BEFORE I'D EVEN LIVED ONE DAY.

ROMANS 5:5 (AMPC)

SUCH HOPE NEVER DISAPPOINTS OR DELUDES OR SHAMES US, FOR GOD'S LOVE HAS BEEN POURED OUT IN OUR HEARTS
THROUGH THE HOLY SPIRIT WHO HAS BEEN GIVEN TO US.

• •••

Stop! Look back! See how God carried you, protected you and brought to this place.
Give Him the praise!

_____

_____

_____

_____

LOVE CHANGES EVERYTHING!!!

PONDER YOUR STEPS!

Drop it!

Seek, and you will find. Ask, and it will be given. Knock, and the door shall be made open. So come on in and dine. Sit your weary self down and hear the Spirit speak so softly and tenderly.

MY daughter, MY saint, MY chosen vessel, and the one I have called MY own, Come into this place and make it your home.

Come in to MY presence when all life's struggles get you down, lay them before ME and pick up your glorious crown.

For you are weary and burdened, when all I want you to be is free, whole and spending this quality time with ME.

Come into this place. Come and lay it down, for what I have for you today can only be found here in MY presence, here at MY feet. So hold open your hands and just begin to receive.

MATHEW 7:7
ASK, AND IT WILL BE GIVEN TO YOU; SEEK, AND YOU WILL FIND;
KNOCK, AND THE DOOR WILL BE OPENED TO YOU.

ISAIAH 62:3 (NIV)
YOU WILL BE A CROWN OF SPLENDOR IN THE LORD'S HAND, A ROYAL DIADEM IN THE HAND OF YOUR GOD.

WHAT CAN YOU DROP TO GO UP FURTHER IN GOD?

I will lay down _____. I will pick up_____.

I will lay down _____. I will pick up_____.

I will lay down _____. I will pick up_____.

I will lay down_____. I will pick up _____.

ASK
SEEK
KNOCK

U CAN Choose

You, MY child, can **CHOOSE** to live life full or allow the ways of this world to leave you with a thirst.

It is by **CHOICE** you decide to walk in peace, joy and MY presence.

It's in these quiet times I am able to pour myself heavy upon you and fill you full to go forth in this world.

It's in these peaceful times I can speak to your heart.

So **CHOOSE** ME today. **CHOOSE** that quiet place if only for a moment and allow MY love to penetrate deep in your soul and fill you full.

Let ME heal the wounds and the fear of rejection you face.

Let MY Spirit take you by the hand and guide you to that quiet place to fill you up and send you out!

You CHOOSE.

DEUTERONOMY 30:19 (NIV)

THIS DAY I CALL THE HEAVENS AND THE EARTH AS WITNESSES AGAINST YOU THAT I HAVE SET BEFORE YOUR LIFE AND DEATH, BLESSINGS AND CURSES. NOW CHOOSE LIFE, SO THAT YOU AND YOUR CHILDREN MAY LIVE.

ARE YOU CHOOSING RIGHT?

GOD	SATAN
quiets u	rushes u
reassures u	frightens u
leads u	pushes u
enlightens u	confuses u
forgives u	condemns u
calms u	stresses u
encourages u	discourages u
comforts u	worries u

How do you see these things in your life?

_____

_____

_____

_____

JUST LISTEN. THEN WRITE.

_____

_____

_____

_____

_____

_____

_____

_____

_____

_____

Run Like A River

Let the love of God be shed abroad in your heart. Let it flow freely and never stop!

Let the rivers of living water flow here and there, deep and slow, rapids everywhere.

Let MY love consume your whole being. Let it run so deep and so wide wherever that you go MY, love is your guide.

Put on the garments of praise. Lift up your hands and rejoice in MY love.

Open your hands. Open your heart. Receive freely, MY child. Receive MY heart, for it beats hard. And it beats fast, for it is you I am running after.

Let it flow. Let it go deep and watch how your life unfolds and transforms into the likeness of ME. Let it run like a river. Let it run deep.

JOHN 7:38 (NLT)
ANYONE WHO BELIEVES IN ME MAY COME AND DRINK! FOR THE SCRIPTURES DECLARE,
'RIVERS OF LIVING WATER WILL FLOW FROM HIS HEART.'

SPLASH SOME COLOR ON ME!

ISAIAH 61:3

TO CONSOLE THOSE WHO

MOURN IN ZION.

TO GIVE THEM

BEAUTY FOR ASHES.

THE OIL OF JOY FOR MOURNING.

THE GARMENT OF PRAISE FOR

THE SPIRIT OF HEAVINESS:

THAT THEY MAY BE CALLED

TREES OF RIGHTEOUSNESS.

THE PLANTING OF THE LORD.

THAT HE MAY BE GLORIFIED.

SPEAK THIS OUT LOUD...

LOVE....
LOVE guides me
LOVE showers me
LOVE covers me
LOVE cleanses me
LOVE forgives me
LOVE strengthens me
LOVE clothes me
LOVE redeems me
LOVE sanctifies me
LOVE never fails me
LOVE protects me
LOVE gives to me
LOVE never gives up on me
Jesus LOVES me
GOD IS LOVE

GOD LOVES _____.
LISTEN TO HIS VOICE!

_____

_____

_____

_____

_____

_____

_____

_____

_____

You're not Missing Out

Find a quiet place, and stay here a while. Lay your weary head back and breathe deeply and quietly with ME.

Forget about all the chatter and the things in this world and put your trust in ME and stay a while.

You look around and feel like you're missing out, but really, child, you're exactly where you need to be.

It's here in MY presence, sitting close and listening. Isn't it ME you're going after? Then why get up and leave?

Press in, press in even more, and hear ME whisper. I love you. It's you I adore. You don't need a loud and noisy room with clatter all around. Only you and ME sitting here quietly, enjoying each other.

My daughter, MY princess, I see you are adorned with diamonds and jewels and clothed in royalty.

So, be still. Be still and wait for ME. Just sit here quietly. Sit here with ME and know you are exactly where you need to be.

COLOSSIANS 3:12 (THE MESSAGE)
SO, CHOSEN BY GOD FOR THIS NEW LIFE OF LOVE, DRESS IN THE WARDROBE GOD PICKED OUT
FOR YOU: COMPASSION, KINDNESS, HUMILITY, QUIET STRENGTH, DISCIPLINE.

YOU FEEL LIKE YOU'RE MISSING OUT?

MAYBE NOT! MAYBE YOU'RE EXACTLY WHERE YOU NEED TO BE!

WHAT DO YOU FEEL LIKE YOU'RE MISSING?

_____

_____

_____

_____

THE YOUNG LIONS LACK AND SUFFER HUNGER: BUT THOSE

WHO _____ THE _____ SHALL NOT

_____ ANY _____   _____.

PSALM 34:10

Look Up & See

Look up to ME. Look up when all you feel like doing is looking down.

Go against whatever you're feeling, whatever your emotions are trying to tell you.

Look up to ME, for that is where your heart needs to be.

This world is driven by feelings, emotions of all kinds. But when you are led out by MY Spirit, there is where you can really shine.

All of MY promises are true. MY Word is the final authority. So let it run through you pushing away from the senses and sensual desires in you.

Child, find comfort in ME. Find comfort in MY presence and truly believe. Come to that secret place. Come sit close with ME. Raise your eyes to heaven and look up to ME.

HEBREW 12:2 (NLT)
WE DO THIS BY KEEPING OUR EYES ON JESUS, THE CHAMPION WHO INITIATES AND PERFECTS
OUR FAITH. BECAUSE OF THE JOY AWAITING HIM, HE ENDURED THE CROSS, DISREGARDING ITS SHAME.
NOW HE IS SEATED IN THE PLACE OF HONOR BESIDE GOD'S THRONE..

Ask God! What great attributes does He see in you! How about write them out?

_____

_____

_____

_____

_____

Write out Psalm 91:1 from the Amplified Bible!

_____

_____

_____

_____

_____

Ask God! What great attributes does He see in you!

JUST LISTEN.

_____

_____

_____

_____

_____

_____

_____

_____

Soak

This is MY time now. This is MY time to shine and give you the details of the day.

Sit quietly before ME. Soak in MY presence, and even though you might not "feel ME," KNOW I am here. I AM showing you the way. All you need to do is acknowledge MY presence, speak a word or two and watch how the steps in front open as we walk two-by-two.

MY love for you is deep. MY plans for you are grand. So believe in every step you take. These are the ones laid securely in place.

But remember, MY child. Remember! Seek ME and ask ME. I will not lead you astray. And if you get off course, don't run away. But just step back and let ME show you the way.

It's a lifetime of changes, challenges and growing in ME. But always believe MY love never changes and MY ways are true. So don't get sidetracked and follow the crowds. Get quietly before ME, and I will give you all the details.

So listen, MY child, listen to ME today. Soak in MY presence. Lay everything down.

If only for a moment, come and lay your burdens down.

Let ME just love on you a while, fill you full and then send you out!

MATTHEW 7:7 (NLT)
KEEP ON ASKING, AND YOU WILL RECEIVE WHAT YOU ASK FOR. KEEP ON SEEKING,
AND YOU WILL FIND. KEEP ON KNOCKING, AND THE DOOR WILL BE OPENED TO YOU.

PSALM 37:23
THE STEPS OF A GOOD MAN ARE ORDERED BY THE LORD.
AND HE DELIGHTS IN HIS WAY.

God wants to hear your heart and know your passions. He wants to know YOU.
Lay it out!

Your...

heart _____

passions _____

pain _____

confession _____

NOW LISTEN...

_____

_____

_____

_____

How Deep Is Your Love?

It is in MY presence you begin to change, close beside ME, worshiping, talking and being with ME. There you will be transformed into the image of ME.

MY beloved, MY great love for you draws you to ME. Just open your heart and receive it all from ME.

MY love is deep and never runs dry. MY heart pounds in love for you, MY child, and this is not a lie. Receive all I have for you. Receive it with a glad heart, watch your life transform and watch your surroundings light up.

MY love is strong, stable and true. MY love will never change. MY love is deep and true.

So come into MY presence and lay all your burdens down. Listen to MY heart speak.

Child, come lay it all down. Receive! That's all I ask from you. Receive MY glorious, never-changing love. Receive, for its all here for you.

MY love is deep, deep in love with you.

EPHESIANS 3:18-19
MAY BE ABLE TO COMPREHEND WITH ALL THE SAINTS WHAT IS THE WIDTH AND
LENGTH AND DEPTH AND HEIGHT TO KNOW THE LOVE OF CHRIST WHICH PASSES KNOWLEDGE:
THAT YOU MAY BE FILLED WITH ALL THE FULLNESS OF GOD.

SPEAK IT OUT! WRITE IT OUT!

GOD LOVES ME.

GOD IS FOR ME.

GOD LOVES ME.

GOD WILL NEVER LEAVE ME.

GOD LOVES ME.

_____

_____

_____

IF YOU'RE ASKING if I need you.
The answer is forever!
IF YOU'RE ASKING IF I'LL LEAVE YOU,
The answer is never!
IF YOU'RE ASKING WHAT I VALUE,
The answer is YOU!
If you're asking IF I LOVE YOU,
THE ANSWER IS I DO.

Stacey Berry

Scribble your thoughts!

The Guide On The Inside

ZACHARIAH 4:6
NOT BY MIGHT, NOT BY POWER, BUT BY MY SPIRIT, SAYS THE LORD.

It is MY Spirit who will guide you in all truth and in all your ways. So trust ME with your whole heart and believe you are moving forth in the direction I have made for you.

When you feel confused and out of sorts, just stop and pray. I will give you the instruction, I will lead the way.

The more you lean on ME and the more you follow MY lead, the deeper you will go. The more you will see and the more you will know.

So trust ME today and allow ME to take you places I see fit. Allow MY Spirit to guide you, show you and teach you MY ways.

All this time is not wasted time, child, but only preparation and training to build you up strong, mighty, fearless and bold. For MY love for you is beyond your control. MY heart is full and overflowing for you. So child, hear me say,

NOT by might, not by power, but by MY Spirit. MY Spirit will lead the way!

PROVERBS 3:5-6 (AMPC)
LEAN ON, TRUST IN, AND BE CONFIDENT IN THE LORD WITH ALL YOUR HEART
AND MIND AND DO NOT RELY ON YOUR OWN INSIGHT OR UNDERSTANDING.
IN ALL YOUR WAYS KNOW, RECOGNIZE, AND ACKNOWLEDGE
HIM, AND HE WILL DIRECT AND MAKE STRAIGHT AND PLAIN YOUR PATHS.

PSALM 25:4-5

_____ ME YOUR WAYS, O LORD;

_____ ME YOUR PATHS.

_____ ME IN YOUR _____ AND _____ ME, FOR YOU ARE GOD OF
MY SALVATION; ON YOU I WAIT ALL THE WAY.

WHERE ARE YOU GOING? LET GOD LEAD YOU TODAY!

_____

_____

_____

_____

_____

Love Comes And Goes

Love conquers all.
Love drives away fear.
Love brings confidence, strength and peace to your soul.
Love never fails....

Love comes and goes depending on your feelings.

Love is an emotion sometimes confused with lust, idolatry and self. But, child, with MY love, there is no end.

MY people try to love with their own hearts, but you must first receive the love I have for you in order to give such an abundance away.

Love will destroy the yoke of bondage. Love will cover a multitude of sins. MY love is beyond comprehension to most, and some really never receive all I have for them.

But you must learn to walk in MY love. Connect with ME on a deeper level. Come to this place and listen for MY voice. Feel the touch of MY Spirit. Be still and allow the love of MY heart to overflow.

I love you, MY child. Begin to say every day: "The love of the Father is in me. The love of God has me in the palm of HIS hand, and HE will never leave me, never forsake me."

Get to that place where you truly believe, and then you will begin to move mountains. You will walk confidently in ME.

Let MY love run deep, and then you will see, you are a child of the Almighty God, almighty indeed.

1 JOHN 4:16 AMPC
AND WE KNOW (UNDERSTAND, RECOGNIZE, ARE CONSCIOUS OF, BY OBSERVATION AND BY EXPERIENCE) AND BELIEVE (ADHERE TO AND PUT FAITH IN AND RELY ON) THE LOVE GOD CHERISHES FOR US. GOD IS LOVE, AND HE WHO DWELLS AND CONTINUES IN LOVE DWELLS AND CONTINUES IN GOD, AND GOD DWELLS AND CONTINUES IN HIM.

1 JOHN 3:16 (AMPC)
BY THIS WE COME TO KNOW (PROGRESSIVELY TO RECOGNIZE, TO PERCEIVE, TO UNDERSTAND) THE [ESSENTIAL] LOVE: THAT HE LAID DOWN HIS [OWN] LIFE FOR US; AND WE OUGHT TO LAY [OUR] LIVES DOWN FOR [THOSE WHO ARE OUR] BROTHERS IN HIM.

- -

LOVE

HE HOLDS US IN HIS LOVING EMBRACE, AND NOTHING CAN COME BETWEEN US.
ABSOLUTELY NOTHING.
NOT TODAY. NOT TOMORROW.
NOT IN THIS LIFE OR THE NEXT.
THERE ARE NO WORDS, NO FORCES, NO FEELINGS, NO ACTIONS —
NOTHING THAT CAN SEPARATE US FROM HIS LOVE.

Open your heart and write something!

_____

_____

_____

_____

_____

_____

_____

_____

_____

_____

_____

_____

Dear Daughter,

You don't mean ANYTHING to me.
You mean EVERYTHING to me.

Love, God

In An Instant

In an instant the life you now know can change from the darkness to become the light of the world.

Write, MY child, write what I say, for in an instant it all could fade away.
Your dreams, visions and heart's desires are all in the palm of MY hand, being set on fire, for MY mighty and grand plan.

Just remember when life begins to change, you must keep your focus, your attention on ME. You, MY child, are the apple of MY eye — a precious jewel, a beautiful design made for MY glory and ready to go forth and shine.

  So let your heart be open and your mind alert, for the life you now see and know, can all be changed in an instant, in a twinkling of an eye.

ISAIAH 49:16
SEE, I HAVE INSCRIBED YOU ON THE PALMS OF MY HANDS; YOUR WALLS ARE CONTINUALLY BEFORE ME.

WELL, DO WHAT IT SAYS! WRITE!
What is God speaking to you today?
ASK HIM TO REVEAL HIMSELF TO YOU!

_____

_____

_____

_____

_____

_____

_____

_____

_____

_____

Eye Of The Storm

In the midst of the storm, remember who has called you by name. In the eye of the hurricane, know who is standing by your side.

In this life you will have fires, storms and trials. In this world you will find hurt, doubt and unkindness.

But, MY daughter, when you know the love I have poured out for you, the love I have given, you can look at the storm or the havoc of life and just say, "Everything will be all right!"

God is MY Savior and MY Light. HE will guide me through and keep me on course. MY God and MY King loves me so. Nothing in this world will stop HIS flow.

God so loved the world HE gave HIS only Son. This is for all; this is for everyone. So when the storms come and you feel stressed, remember, MY love: Come into MY arms, and there you will find rest

JAMES 1:2 (THE MESSAGE)

CONSIDER IT A SHEER GIFT, FRIENDS, WHEN TESTS AND CHALLENGES COME AT YOU FROM ALL SIDES. YOU KNOW THAT UNDER PRESSURE, YOUR FAITH-LIFE IS FORCED INTO THE OPEN AND SHOWS ITS TRUE COLORS. SO DON'T TRY TO GET OUT OF ANYTHING PREMATURELY. LET IT DO ITS WORK SO YOU BECOME MATURE AND WELL-DEVELOPED, NOT DEFICIENT IN ANY WAY.

JOHN 3:16

FOR GOD SO LOVED THE WORLD THAT HE GAVE HIS ONLY BEGOTTEN SON, THAT WHOEVER BELIEVES IN HIM SHOULD NOT PERISH BUT HAVE EVERLASTING LIFE.

Are you in the middle of a trial or a storm?
Come before the Father and lay it all down.

_____

_____

_____

God has a GOOD WORD for you! Get in it! Read it! What is it saying to you?

Psalm 107:28-31 _____

Psalm 55:6-8 _____

Nahum 1:7 NLT _____

Psalm 27:4-6 _____

Psalm 9:9-10 _____

Joshua 1:9 _____

JOT IT DOWN!

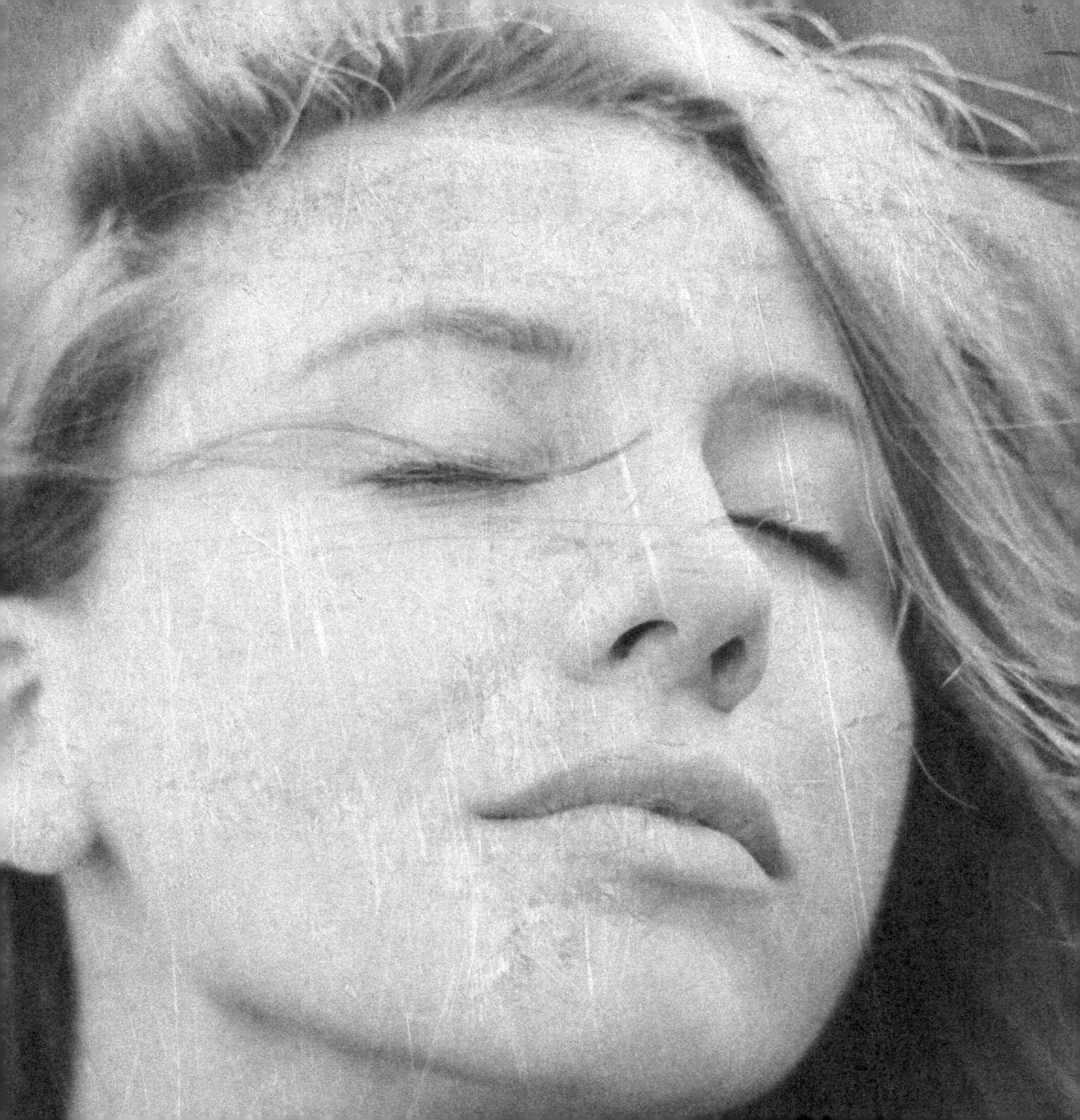

Dreams Do Come True

Dream, MY child. Dream your little dreams. Let your imagination go wild. Let it flow from within. For when the time comes, those dreams will expand, and they will grow.

Follow your heart. Follow those dreams, but always put ME first and watch the impossible be redeemed. MY hand is on you. MY Spirit is guiding you through.

So dream, MY child, dream. For dreams will always come true when you look unto ME. I will see them through.

PSALM 37:4 (AMPC)
DELIGHT YOURSELF ALSO IN THE LORD, AND HE WILL GIVE YOU
THE DESIRES AND SECRET PETITIONS OF YOUR HEART.

What's the dream God has placed in your heart? Is it too big to believe or too small and easy to accomplish?

BE BOLD. ASK HIM.

HE'S GOT THE ANSWERS.

Do You Have What it Takes?

DO YOU HAVE THE PASSION, THE DRIVE?

DO YOU HAVE THE DISCIPLINE AND HEART TO MAKE IT WORK?

ARE YOU WILLING TO PUT ALL OF YOU ASIDE AND LET THE SPIRIT ON THE INSIDE BE YOUR TRUE GUIDE?

DO YOU HAVE IT?

Do you have what it takes?

It's not by might, nor by power, but by MY Spirit you will rise. It's not by might you will win the prize, nor the one with the most power, but the crown is set for those who are led by MY Spirit. Yes, she is the one who will win the mighty crown.

Get off the emotional roller coaster and the turmoil from within. Move away from the rejection and despair that you feel.

Come on, MY friend. Come work it out with ME. Come boldly to the throne room. Come and find all the grace you will need.

You DO have all MY attributes, all of ME on the inside, but you must first let the Spirit guide, the One who lives on the inside.

ROMANS 8:14 (NLT)
FOR ALL WHO ARE LED BY THE SPIRIT OF GOD ARE CHILDREN OF GOD.

HEBREWS 4:16 (NLT)
SO LET US COME BOLDLY TO THE THRONE OF OUR GRACIOUS GOD. THERE WE WILL RECEIVE HIS MERCY,
AND WE WILL FIND GRACE TO HELP US WHEN WE NEED IT MOST.

WHAT'S YOUR PASSION?
WHAT DRIVES YOU EACH DAY?
YOU HAVE WHAT IT TAKES!

JOURNAL IT!

_____

_____

_____

_____

_____

_____

_____

Orchestrated Time

Since the beginning of time, I have called you, handpicked you and said you are MY own.

It was there I saw you and said, "She is MINE. I have plans, dreams and desires for her." It was before the foundation of this world that I chose you! I have made the way clear. I have ordered your steps, and I have marked the way.

Now I say, WALK IN IT! I have set your steps solid in the place I have laid. Now watch your life unfold. Watch and see each door open wide for you.

My dear, I have called you from afar. I have placed MY mighty hand upon you, and all I ask from you is to walk forth, trust ME and see. The plans I have for you are mighty indeed.

So be ready, willing and full of joy, for your ways are ordered and ordained before the foundation of time. They are orchestrated and finely tuned by the Almighty God!

JEREMIAH 29:11 (NIV)
FOR I KNOW THE PLANS I HAVE FOR YOU," DECLARES THE LORD, "PLANS TO PROSPER YOU
AND NOT TO HARM YOU, PLANS TO GIVE YOU HOPE AND A FUTURE.

PSALM 139:16 (THE MESSAGE)
LIKE AN OPEN BOOK, YOU WATCH ME GROW FROM CONCEPTION TO BIRTH; ALL THE STAGES OF MY LIFE WERE SPREAD
OUT BEFORE YOU, THE DAYS OF MY LIFE ALL PREPARED BEFORE I'D EVEN LIVED ONE DAY.

How do you fit into God's orchestra?

_____

What instrument would you be? Why?

_____

_____

WRITE A LOVE SONG OR POEM TO HIM!

_____

_____

_____

_____

WALK IT OUT!

Just listen and write!

_____

_____

_____

_____

_____

_____

_____

_____

_____

_____

_____

Praise On Your Lips

Sing a song of **praise**. Sing a song today. Lift up your voice. Lift up your **praise** for the God Almighty, glorious and all, has called you-MY redeemed, full of glory, splendor and royalty.

So sing a song of **praise**, MY child. Sing with all your heart, for you are the beloved, chosen from the very start.

Psalm 138:1-2 (NIV) I will praise you, LORD, with all my heart; before the "gods" I will sing your praise.

I will bow down toward your holy temple and will praise your name for your unfailing love and your faithfulness, for you have so exalted your solemn decree that it surpasses your fame.

PSALM 19:14
LET THE WORDS OF MY MOUTH AND THE MEDITATIONS OF MY HEART
BE PLEASING TO YOU, O LORD, MY ROCK AND MY REDEEMER.

TODAY...PUT ON YOUR
FAVORITE WORSHIP MUSIC
AND JUST GIVE HIM PRAISE!

Twisted Love

In this life you will face trouble — darkness all around.

But, child, when you open your heart up to ME, then you will see the truth. You will see the true light shining in the earth.

MY love is for all who will reach out their hands.

MY love will come forth in a way no one has ever seen, but you must open up your heart. Open up your hands and receive.

Love has been twisted, turned and used in ways to break people's hearts and deceive them into following things in the dark.

The love the world has will deceive, lie and pull people away. We need to show them MY love, MY heart and the One True God!

I AM love. I AM the One who created it. MY love is never ending. There are, no strings attached and nothing on your part but to receive, only to grab hold and take!

So, child, receive MY love. Take it all in and watch your life transform.
MY love will never change. You only need to believe, and when you truly receive, you are able to take it by faith and love like ME...unconditionally.

1 JOHN 4:16
AND WE HAVE KNOWN AND BELIEVED THE LOVE THAT GOD HAS FOR US. GOD IS LOVE.
AND HE WHO ABIDES IN LOVE ABIDES IN GOD, AND GOD IN HIM.

ECCLESIASTES 4:12 (NLT)
A PERSON STANDING ALONE CAN BE ATTACKED AND DEFEATED. BUT TWO CAN STAND BACK-TO-BACK AND CONQUER. THREE ARE EVEN BETTER, FOR A TRIPLE-BRAIDED CORD IS NOT EASILY BROKEN.

1 JOHN 3:1 (THE MESSAGE)
WHAT MARVELOUS LOVE THE FATHER HAS EXTENDED TO US! JUST LOOK AT IT WE'RE CALLED CHILDREN OF GOD! THAT'S WHO WE REALLY ARE. BUT THAT'S ALSO WHY THE WORLD DOESN'T RECOGNIZE US OR TAKE US SERIOUSLY, BECAUSE IT HAS NO IDEA WHO HE IS OR WHAT HE'S UP TO.

TWiSTED

What would your life look like if you knew without any doubt that God loves you completely, totally and fiercely? Do you believe it now?

_____

_____

_____

_____

"His love has no limits, His grace has no measure. His power no boundary known unto men. For out of His infinite riches in Jesus, He giveth and giveth and giveth again."

Annie Johnson Flint
1866-1932

Has the enemy twisted love in your life? How? Now bring it to God. Let Him reveal to you how His love can heal, restore and make you clean.

_____

_____

_____

_____

_____

_____

_____

_____

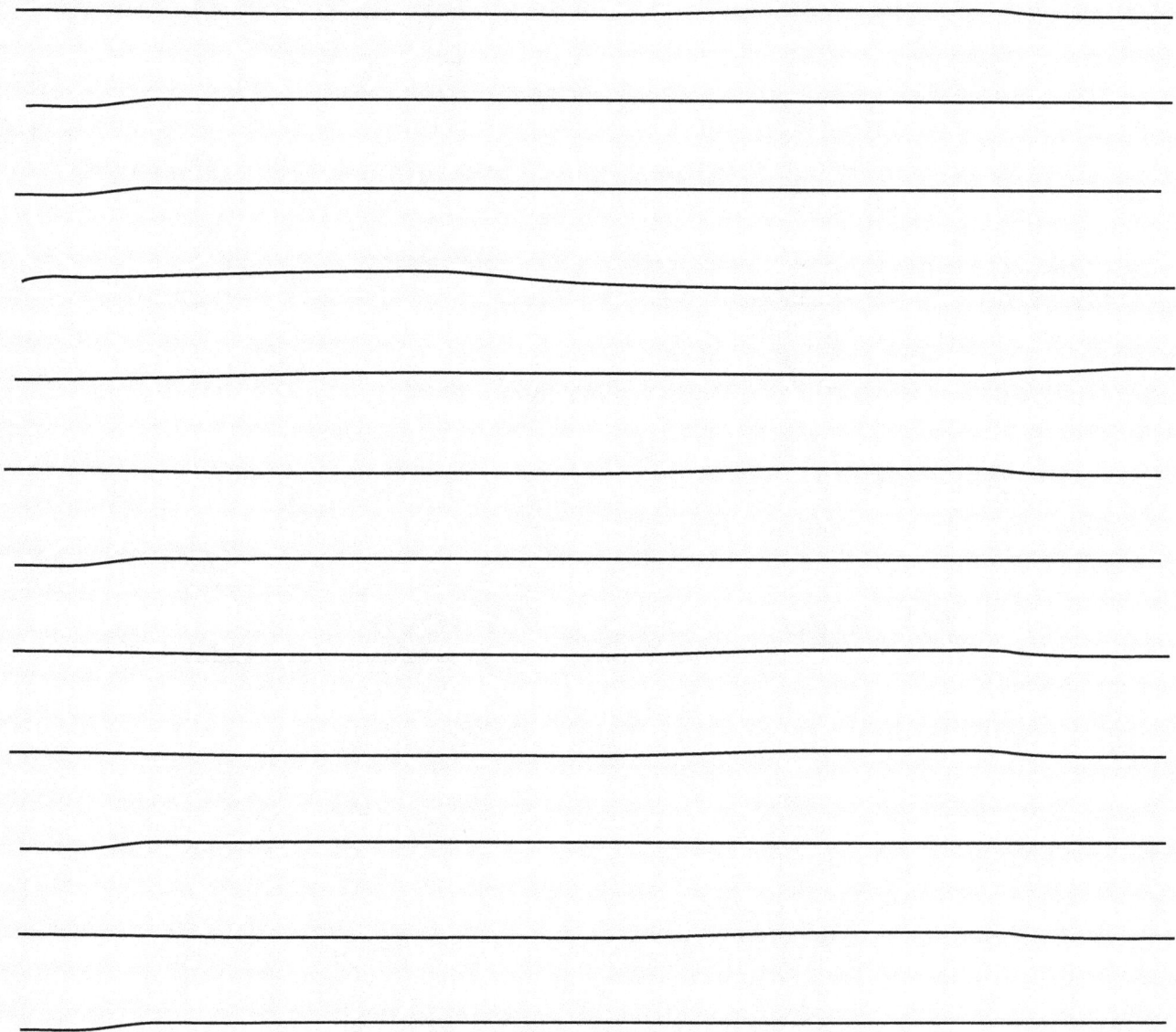

There Is A Perfect Love

Perfect love casts out fear. **MY love** is perfect. **MY love** will cast out all fear, anxiety and stress when you rest in ME.

Rest quietly in MY presence. Come to that secret place with ME. When you place yourself deep within that place, then all life's issues are pushed aside, and fear subsides. You are quieted with ME.

So, My child, rest in ME. Come experience **MY love** and MY goodness in a new and refreshing way.

Come to that secret place and hear ME say today: rest, be still and quiet yourself. Let **My love** run deep and quiet you still.

MY love is perfect. MY love is real!

1 JOHN 4:17-18 (THE MESSAGE)
GOD IS LOVE. WHEN WE TAKE UP PERMANENT RESIDENCE IN A LIFE OF LOVE. WE LIVE IN GOD AND GOD LIVES IN US. THIS WAY. LOVE HAS THE RUN OF THE HOUSE. BECOMES AT HOME AND MATURE IN US. SO THAT WE'RE FREE OF WORRY ON JUDGMENT DAY OUR STANDING IN THE WORLD IS IDENTICAL WITH CHRIST'S. THERE IS NO ROOM IN LOVE FOR FEAR. WELL-FORMED LOVE BANISHES FEAR. SINCE FEAR IS CRIPPLING. A FEARFUL LIFE FEAR OF DEATH. FEAR OF JUDGMENT IS ONE NOT YET FULLY FORMED IN LOVE.

PSALM 46:10 (NLT)
BE STILL. AND KNOW THAT I AM GOD!

There is no perfect love away from Him!

PARK YOURSELF SOMEWHERE. WHAT DOES THAT SECRET PLACE LOOK LIKE TO YOU? WHO IS GOD TO YOU?

What Matters? Worship!

Sight and sounds, bells and balls, a loud clang, a way to **worship** it all.

Let the praise begin, and let it fall on you. Open your heart. and let it burst out of you. Harp or flute, drums to a heavy beat — it doesn't matter to ME. Just come and **worship** ME.

Whether it's loud or soft, or quiet still, come into MY presence. Come and be still. This is a time to **worship**, a time to give ME your all.

So lay aside the burdens. Lay aside the call and come today. Come and **worship** ME and walk away full, blessed and anointed still. But overflowing to those all around, flooding MY love over all of them!

PSALM 150:3-5 (NIV)
PRAISE HIM WITH THE SOUNDING OF THE TRUMPET. PRAISE HIM WITH THE HARP AND LYRE.
PRAISE HIM WITH TIMBREL AND DANCING. PRAISE HIM WITH THE STRINGS AND PIPE.
PRAISE HIM WITH THE CLASH OF CYMBALS.
PRAISE HIM WITH RESOUNDING CYMBALS.

WHAT DOES WORSHIP LOOK LIKE TO YOU?

UR
MY GOD.
I WILL PRAISE U.
UR
MY GOD,
I WILL
EXALT U.

JUST DO IT! JUST WORSHIP HIM!

WRITE IT!
SING IT!
DANCE TO IT!

JUST DO IT!

Write it!

_____

_____

_____

_____

_____

_____

_____

_____

_____

_____

REFLECT YOUR TIME OF WORSHIP...

It's Really Cool. Look Up!

Glory, splendor and all majesty.

Full of great and mighty glory for the world to see.

Mountains and hills, valleys and such, oh what a sight for the world to see. What a magnificent view. If only MY creation would look up!

Look up and see MY hand so mighty. This beauty I have created for you, full of power, majesty and super cool!

So lay things aside and just look out—the birds, the bees, the leaves on the trees. This I made. This I have done for all of MY creation, for all of MY loved ones.

Enjoy it all today, the glory the splendor all I have made.

Enjoy. Enjoy. Enjoy it all today!

PSALM 145:5
I WILL MEDITATE ON THE GLORIOUS SPLENDOR OF
YOUR MAJESTY, AND ON YOUR WONDROUS WORKS.

GOD IS COOL, AND HE LIVES IN YOU!

GO OUTSIDE ON PURPOSE. LOOK UP! SEE GOD'S MARVELOUS HAND IN EVERYTHING. WHAT DID YOU SEE?

_____

_____

_____

_____

No Matter What

No matter what you see, no matter what you hear, press in, press in to ME.

The more the darkness tries to climb, the more MY light will shine.

Although this world is full of darkness, hostility and rules, MY grace is sufficient. MY love overrules.

MY children I have called. MY saints I have chosen, so, dear child, know and believe MY love will conquer it all.

No matter what you see, no matter what you hear, MY Spirit is always leading, guiding you along the path of life. All you need to do is grab hold and don't shrink back!

MY love is always here. Reach out. Grab hold. And never fear!

JOHN 1:5
AND THE LIGHT SHINES IN THE DARKNESS, AND THE DARKNESS DID NOT COMPREHEND IT.

GALATIANS 5:25
IF WE LIVE IN THE SPIRIT, LET US ALSO WALK IN THE SPIRIT.

3 FEARS THAT TRY TO STOP YOU

———————

———————

———————

HOW LOVE OVERTAKES....

WRITE OUT 3 SCRIPTURES THAT SHOW GOD'S
LOVE WILL OVERTAKE THOSE FEARS!

I CAN _____ (Philippians 4:13)

_____

_____

_____

_____

_____

Scribble your thoughts!

Seek The Finer Things

Seek the finer things in life. **Seek** those hidden things.

I have gifts that sometimes can't be seen; they can be hidden away. You must **seek** first MY kingdom, and then oh how surprised your heart will be!

I have gifts and talents laid deep down inside. But you must **seek** them and soon they will arrive. MY plans for you are grand, bigger than you can dream. But you must stop looking down and start looking up to ME.

You, MY child, are blessed, anointed and free. You have been called to walk in this life close and beside ME.

So today I say lay everything down. Let go of the darkness, the chains and fear all around. Come to that quiet place. Come sit with ME and listen closely.

Seek the finer things, child. **Seek** after ME!

MATTHEW 6:33
BUT SEEK FIRST THE KINGDOM OF GOD AND HIS RIGHTEOUSNESS, AND ALL THESE THINGS SHALL BE ADDED TO YOU.

JEREMIAH 29:13
AND YOU WILL SEEK ME AND FIND ME, WHEN YOU SEARCH FOR ME WITH ALL YOUR HEART.

```
S J O V E R C O M E R U P W L
V S R E T H G U A D R U A C L
I I E F O R G I V E N T N Z I
C P N N C H I L D O F G O D H
T D R H S B L E S S E D I I A
O E X I I U E U U I D T N B N
R I T X E M O O F E H H T E O
I F F E E S I E I I E G E L Y
O I S D L C T F T R T L D I T
U L S U E P I H I H O U E E I
S A G R S T M T O V G E A V C
Q U P V C E E O E O R I T E B
U Q X N X D J D C F D T R R B
E D A M Y L L U F R E D N O W
O S C D D E I F I T S U J W W
```

— — — — — — — — — — — — — — —

ANOINTED
BEAUTIFUL
BELIEVER
BLESSED
CHILDOFGOD
CITYONAHILL
COMPLETE
DAUGHTER
FORGIVEN

FREE
OVERCOMER
PRECIOUS
PRIESTHOOD
PURE
QUALIFIED
REDEEMED
HIS
INHERITED

INHIM
JESUS
JUSTIFIED
LOVED
SANCTIFIED
VICTORIOUS
WONDERFULLY MADE

It's My Part, Not Yours

Although you don't see the end from the beginning, I do! I see it all; I see who you really are. I see the woman I have created you to be, strong, mighty and full of MY glory.

I have no rules, no stipulation you need to follow; only believe in ME and give your heart away, child.

The love I have is above your knowledge, but I AM able to show you daily as I pour MY love deeper in you.

So breathe in MY goodness. Walk forth in MY joy, and receive the great and mighty love I have for you.

You don't need to do anything but receive. When you do, you will begin to see what I see, for I see the end from the beginning. I see all that's inside of you.

So come. Be blessed. Open your heart to ME. Watch your life expand and your understanding and revelation of ME increase!

I AM full of glory, love and peace, and what's so cool, MY child, is that I live in you!

1 JOHN 4:4 (NIV)
YOU, DEAR CHILDREN, ARE FROM GOD AND HAVE OVERCOME THEM, BECAUSE THE
ONE WHO IS IN YOU IS GREATER THAN THE ONE WHO IS IN THE WORLD.

AND MAY YOU HAVE THE POWER TO UNDERSTAND, AS ALL GOD'S PEOPLE SHOULD, HOW WIDE, HOW LONG, HOW HIGH, AND HOW DEEP HIS LOVE IS. MAY YOU EXPERIENCE THE LOVE OF CHRIST, THOUGH IT IS TOO GREAT TO UNDERSTAND FULLY. THEN YOU WILL BE MADE COMPLETE WITH ALL THE FULLNESS OF LIFE AND POWER THAT COMES FROM GOD.

Ephesians 1:17-23 (NKJV)

That the God of our Lord Jesus Christ, the Father of _____ may give to you the Spirit of _____ and _____ in the _____ of Him. The _____ of my understanding being _____ that you may know what is the _____ of His _____. And what are the riches of the glory of His _____ in the saints and what is the _____ _____ of His power towards us who believe according to the working of His _____ power which He worked in Christ when He raised Him from the dead and seated Him at his hand in _____ places. Far above all _____ and _____ and _____ and _____ and every name that is named not only in this age, but also in that which is to come.

IT'S NOT WHAT YOU DO. IT'S WHO YOU ARE AND WHAT HE HAS DONE. YOU ARE THE RIGHTEOUSNESS OF GOD. HE WILL CLEAN YOU UP AND SEND YOU OUT.

My Word Is Rich

Let the Word of God dwell in you richly. Let it sink down in your soul, and then you'll find peace that you've been looking for.

Let MY Word dwell in you richly. Let it sink down in your soul, for when you find you're thirsty, MY Word will fill you full.

COLOSSIANS 3:16
LET THE WORD OF CHRIST DWELL IN YOU RICHLY IN ALL WISDOM, TEACHING AND ADMONISHING ONE ANOTHER IN PSALMS AND HYMNS AND SPIRITUAL SONGS, SINGING WITH GRACE IN YOUR HEARTS TO THE LORD.

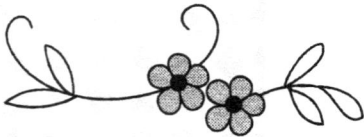

EPHESIANS 1:4 (AMPC)

EVEN AS [IN HIS LOVE] HE CHOSE US [ACTUALLY PICKED US OUT FOR HIMSELF AS HIS OWN] IN CHRIST BEFORE THE FOUNDATION OF THE WORLD, THAT WE SHOULD BE HOLY (CONSECRATED AND SET APART FOR HIM) AND BLAMELESS IN HIS SIGHT, EVEN ABOVE REPROACH, BEFORE HIM IN LOVE.

SCRIBBLE DOWN YOUR OWN WORDS TO GOD.

WHAT DOES IT MEAN TO YOU THAT HE PICKED YOU AND CALLED YOU BEFORE TIME BEGAN?

_____

_____

_____

_____

_____

_____

_____

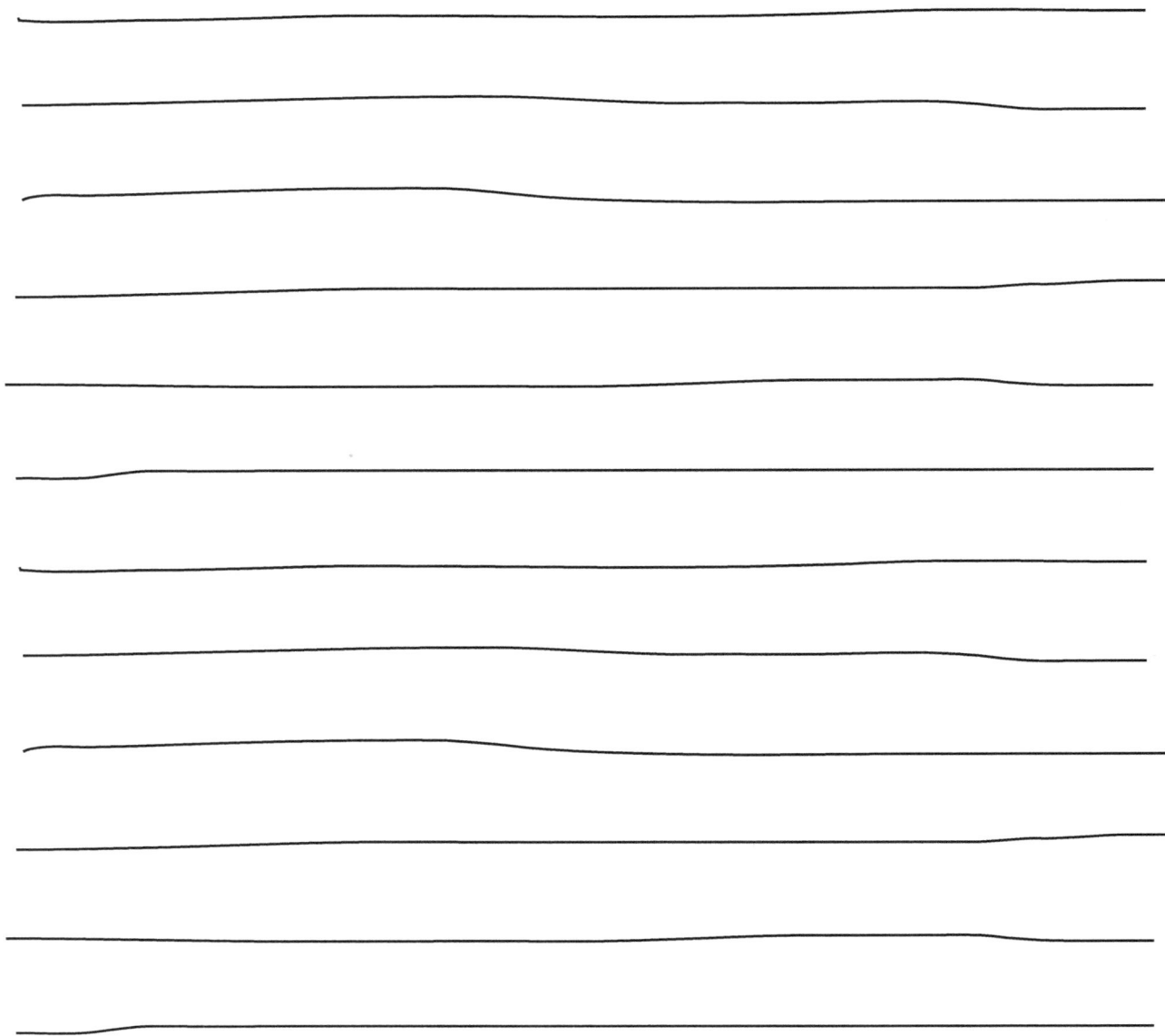

6 W...

7 Our fathers understood not
wonders in...
They remembered not...
...titudes, of thy lovingkindness...
But were rebellious at the sea,
even at the Red Sea.

8 Nevertheless he saved them
for his name's sake,
That he might make his mighty
power to be known.

9 He rebuked the Red Sea also,
and it was dried up:

26 Th...
thou...
therein:

27 These wait all...
thou...
That thou mayest...
their food in due season.

28 Thou givest unto them, they
gather;
Thou openest thy hand, they
are satisfied with good.

29 Thou hidest thy face, they are
troubled;

He shor...

1 Heb. ...
2 Or. ...
1 Or. is stretched out
3 Heb. Jah   4 Heb. the children
5 Another reading is, afflicted me with
strength

BOOK V

Jehovah delivereth Men from Manifold Troubles.

107 O give thanks unto Je-
ho'vah, for he is good:
For his lovingkindness endureth
for ever.

2 Let the redeemed of Je-ho'vah
say so,

Start Playing Your Part

Cast your cares aside. Cast all your burdens down and follow ME. Follow MY lead, and then you will see the path lit brightly beneath your feet.

Stop the chatter, all the negativity. Look up to ME. This is where it starts putting your trust in the things of God and putting your heart with ME.

When you're looking around, looking at others, I don't get the glory! Look to ME for your confidence. Let ME build your self-esteem. I have great dreams that only you can dream.

It's you I have called MY own. It is you I want. So stop looking at those all around. Start playing your own part.

Stop looking at others to fill those empty places in your soul, look to ME—JESUS—I AM the only one who can show you the way.

So come with ME and don't look away, but keep your eyes on ME and listen to what I have to say. This life you live is all about ME and MY glory, not what you see.

So come lay everything down and see all I've called YOU to be.

It is MY time, child, MY time for you to shine. Keep your eyes on ME; that's all that needs to be!

1 PETER 5:7 (AMPC)
CASTING THE WHOLE OF YOUR CARE [ALL YOUR ANXIETIES, ALL YOUR WORRIES, ALL YOUR CONCERNS, ONCE AND FOR ALL] ON HIM, FOR HE CARES FOR YOU AFFECTIONATELY AND CARES ABOUT YOU WATCHFULLY.

CAST YOUR BURDEN ON THE LORD [RELEASING THE WEIGHT OF IT] AND HE WILL SUSTAIN YOU;
HE WILL NEVER ALLOW THE [CONSISTENTLY] RIGHTEOUS TO BE MOVED (MADE TO SLIP, FALL, OR FAIL).

What's your part? Take time to listen. Let Him show you the steps you need to take. Listen to His voice tell you where you fit.

Ephesians 2:10
For we are His _____ created in Christ Jesus, for _____ _____ which God prepared beforehand that we should _____ in them.

Philippians 2:13
For it is _____ who _____ in you both to _____ and to _____ for _____ _____ _____.

Just listen and write!

_____

_____

_____

Just listen!

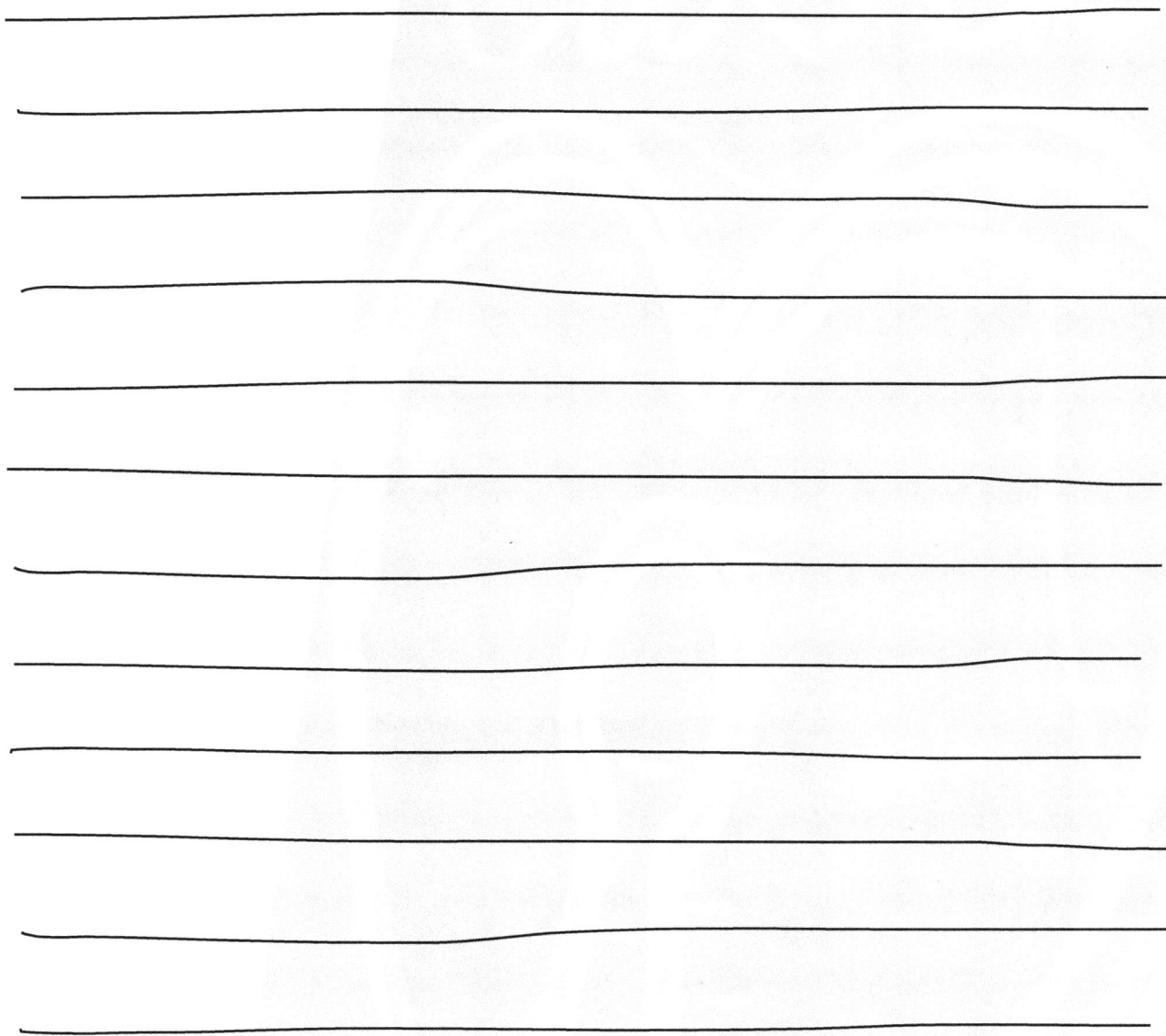

Where Are The Miracles?

God: Signs, wonders and **miracles**, oh how you long to see, the glory of MY Spirit surrounding you and allowing you to be all I've called you to be.

You: Signs, wonders, and miracles, where God did they go? Why don't we see them these days and all you have proclaimed?

God: **Signs, wonders** and **miracles** are all around you MY dear, all you need to do is look up and look near.

God: MY hand is showing you all of MY abundance. MY glory is for you to see, but you must first look up to acknowledge ME. I am here waiting for you to say, God show us your **signs, wonders** and **miracles**. We are hungry for you.

You: We ask today, God, come and blow on us. Come and show up!

You: We believe. We hold fast to all you have spoken, to all you have said.

God: So listen closely to ME. **Signs, wonders** and **miracles** will be for all the world to see. I AM coming fast. I AM here to say, "Look up! Be steadfast, for **signs, wonders** and **miracles** are for all who will ask!"

HEBREW 2:4
GOD ALSO BEARING WITNESS BOTH WITH SIGNS AND WONDERS, WITH VARIOUS
MIRACLES, AND GIFTS OF THE HOLY SPIRIT, ACCORDING TO HIS OWN WILL?

How many miracles can you see today? Ask the Holy Spirit to open your eyes and see His glory all around.

There must be at least one. Write it down.

_____

_____

_____

_____

_____

_____

_____

_____

_____

_____

Lift

Lift up your hands in worship. Lift up your voice in praise. Come to the throne of the Mighty God. Give HIM your all and lift HIM up today.

Come. Place everything down. Lay it down at MY feet. Walk away refreshed, clean and ready for the day.

It's a new time, a time of refreshing, new ideas, and new ways with ME.

So come this day. Lift up your hands in praise. Lift up your voice to heaven and begin this great day!

PSALM 118:24
THIS IS THE DAY THE LORD HAS MADE: WE WILL REJOICE AND BE GLAD IN IT.

PSALM 134:2
LIFT UP YOUR HANDS IN THE SANCTUARY, AND BLESS THE LORD.

The Highest Form Of Worship Is Praise

LOOK UP THESE SCRIPTURES AND WRITE THEM OUT!

PSALM 63:1-5

_____

_____

PSALM 100:1-5

_____

_____

PSALM 44:8

_____

_____

PSALM 47:1-2

_____

_____

Speak From The Heart!

_____

_____

_____

_____

_____

_____

_____

_____

_____

_____

Hardened Shell

It's here in MY presence you come and dwell, ready and waiting for all I AM able to tell.

Come, MY child, and hear ME say, "Today is the day for you to excel!" Open you heart and receive all MY love. Come and let me break through the hardened shell.

Life has taken its toll, with heartaches, wounds and broken-down souls. So when you seek ME today, bring it all in and let ME say, "This is not for you to carry. This is not for you to be heavy laden and weary. I have come to give you life and life more abundantly." So I say, "Freely receive!"

It is all for you, MY daughter. So open your hands. Open your heart and grab hold. Come in MY presence. Come in boldly and say so!

Lay down your burdens and walk away free. This is the place I have called you to be.

MATHEW 11:28 (NIV)
COME TO ME, ALL YOU WHO ARE WEARY AND BURDENED, AND I WILL GIVE YOU REST.

JOHN 10:10 (AMPC)
THE THIEF DOES NOT COME EXCEPT TO STEAL, AND TO KILL, AND TO DESTROY. I HAVE COME
THAT THEY MAY HAVE LIFE, AND THAT THEY MAY HAVE IT MORE ABUNDANTLY

HEBREWS 4:16
LET US THEREFORE COME BOLDLY TO THE THRONE OF GRACE, THAT WE
MAY OBTAIN MERCY AND FIND GRACE TO HELP IN TIME OF NEED.

How do our hearts become hardened? Has yours?
Let God break yours open today!

_____

_____

_____

_____

_____

ALLOW HIM TO PENETRATE YOU WITH HIS LOVE, SO YOU CAN
LEAVE EVERYTHING BEHIND.

IT'S A NEW DAY!
LET HIS LOVE SHINE!

Who Do You Think You Are?

Who do you think you are? What would you say in just one word? Would it be cool or downright rude?

How do you see yourself when you look in the mirror? Ugly, fat or beautiful still? What would you say if I, God Almighty, sat down and asked what you thought? How would you react? Insecure, unworthy and full of lack?

Let me begin this again because, MY dear one, I have things to say. When I look down and look at your face, what would I say in one word or less?

REDEEMED.

That's all it took. MY blood covered the shame, the sin and made you beautiful. You're redeemed and loved, a mighty jewel, a child of the Most High God.

I have crowned you with jewels and robed you with glory. Look at yourself, but this time believe and look in the mirror while you're looking to ME.

Look again and see who you are when you see yourself through ME. Then you see who you really are.

COLOSSIANS 3:12 (AMPC)
CLOTHE YOURSELVES THEREFORE, AS GOD'S OWN CHOSEN ONES (HIS OWN PICKED REPRESENTATIVES), [WHO ARE] PURIFIED AND HOLY AND WELL-BELOVED [BY GOD HIMSELF, BY PUTTING ON BEHAVIOR MARKED BY] TENDERHEARTED PITY AND MERCY, KIND FEELING, A LOWLY OPINION OF YOURSELVES, GENTLE WAYS, [AND] PATIENCE [WHICH IS TIRELESS AND LONG-SUFFERING, AND HAS THE POWER TO ENDURE WHATEVER COMES, WITH GOOD TEMPER].

Read Ephesians 1:1-14

WRITE DOWN WHO U R INCHRIST!

I AM _____

I AM _____

I AM _____

I AM _____

I AM _____

I AM _____

I AM _____

I AM _____

I AM _____

I AM _____

WRITE – REWRITE – MEDITATE

Who U R! > YOU ARE LOVED!

_____

_____

_____

_____

_____

_____

_____

_____

_____

_____

Draw Your Blade

Sometimes you wait, and you feel like it will never be.

But child believe when I say all is well and will soon be all it is meant to be.

Don't be downcast. Don't be full of fear but remember MY words. You are strong and courageous still.

You are called forth into the place I have made. So don't draw back but step in and begin to draw your blade. The weapon you possess is mighty indeed, and when you are ready, many lives you will set free.

So continue to wait with great expectation. Get your hopes up and believe. For the wait is almost over, and the river will run deep.

You are MY precious daughter, the redeemed of the Lord, mighty, holy and full of great glory. You are the one I have called and chosen to go forth.

PSALM 27:14 (AMPC)
WAIT AND HOPE FOR AND EXPECT THE LORD: BE BRAVE AND OF GOOD COURAGE AND LET
YOUR HEART BE STOUT AND ENDURING. YES, WAIT FOR AND HOPE FOR AND EXPECT THE LORD.

EPHESIANS 6:10 (AMPC)
IN CONCLUSION, BE STRONG IN THE LORD [BE EMPOWERED THROUGH YOUR UNION WITH HIM];
DRAW YOUR STRENGTH FROM HIM [THAT STRENGTH WHICH HIS BOUNDLESS MIGHT PROVIDES].

DRESSED TO KILL!

Name your weapons!

_____

_____

_____

PUT ON THE FULL ARMOR OF GOD
— EPH. 6:13-17 NLT

Where are you headed, woman of God?

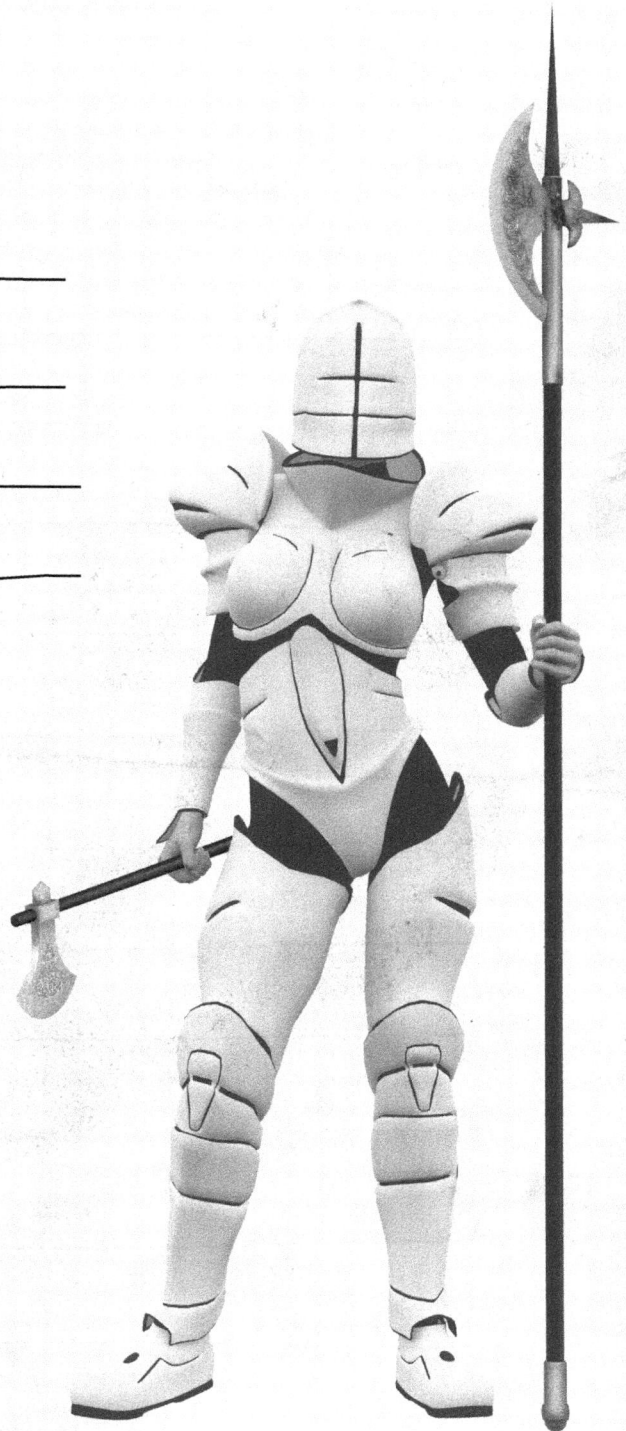

_____

_____

_____

_____

Stop! And just listen again...

_____

_____

_____

_____

_____

_____

_____

_____

_____

_____

Too Big To Plan

It's in these quiet times you hear ME speak. It's in that place of rest you can see the dream.

So place yourself with ME and hold on tight, for MY ways are always higher and much bigger and out of sight.

But when you put all your trust in ME, then you are able to truly see the grand and mighty plan through the eyes of faith, with MY Spirit guiding your way.

So sit quietly with ME today and open your heart and begin to see. I do have a MIGHTY PLAN, a vision too big for human hands. But through ME you can do all things, bigger—stronger and with a heart reaching to receive.

Come today and sit quietly with ME. Let your dreams expand and come and follow ME.

PHILIPPIANS 4:13
I HAVE STRENGTH FOR ALL THINGS IN CHRIST WHO EMPOWERS ME [I AM READY FOR ANYTHING AND EQUAL TO ANYTHING THROUGH HIM WHO INFUSES INNER STRENGTH INTO ME; I AM SELF-SUFFICIENT IN CHRIST'S SUFFICIENCY].

JEREMIAH 29:11 (NIV)
FOR I KNOW THE PLANS I HAVE FOR YOU," DECLARES THE LORD, "PLANS TO PROSPER YOU AND NOT TO HARM YOU, PLANS TO GIVE YOU HOPE AND A FUTURE.

Eph 3:20

Now to _____ who is able to do _____ _____
Above all that we _____ or _____, according to the
_____ that _____ in us.

If you have no limits, then what will you envision or dream?

WRITE IT OUT!

_____

_____

_____

_____

GOTTA PRAY IT OUT!

It's Not Always Easy

It's not always easy, the path that you're on. But when you delight yourself in ME, then you are able to see the light on each path illuminated and brightly lit.

It's a time of refreshing, dwelling close beside ME. Don't be in such a hurry to get ahead of ME. It's in these quiet times of just you and ME when I pour MY Spirit out and fill you full.

My child whom I adore, I have called you forth to step up. Now be the person I've called you to be.

Remember: it's not who **YOU** think you are today it's who **I have said you are to be**. You are mine, redeemed and a precious gem.

Although you don't see the sparkle and shine, it takes time to be refined.

So don't be discouraged. Don't look away but be full of great encouragement and hope. Your steps are making the way firm and steady and solid for ME.

My Spirit is guiding you straight. You're abiding in ME.

PSALM 37:4 (AMPC)
DELIGHT YOURSELF ALSO IN THE LORD, AND HE WILL GIVE YOU
THE DESIRES AND SECRET PETITIONS OF YOUR HEART.

Read Colossians 1:9-14 and Colossians 2:6-10

What do these scriptures say about you?

_____

_____

_____

_____

JOURNAL IT!

_____

_____

_____

_____

_____

Warrior Praise

MY daughter, let ME pour MYSELF in you and fill you full and overflowing with MY Spirit and MY love. Allow ME to penetrate deep down in your heart.

Let go of the lies. Let go of the false words and hear ME speak to you today.

You are a child of the Most High God, beautiful, precious and full of MY glory. Allow the joy of MY heart to go deep down in your soul. Receive it now in MY name. Receive all I have for you.

Don't allow the voice of the enemy to pull you away. Don't listen to the lies and things he tries to say. Listen to ME, my beautiful child. Listen to ME today. You are strong in ME. You are MY warrior of praise, and you will conquer this battle. So don't lose hope, but get up and know I AM fighting the battle for you.

I AM sending MY angels now over you. Enjoy MY love, MY goodness. Rest in MY presence, for here is where you will win the battle. Here is where you will be refreshed, energized and made new.

So come now to the secret place of the Most High. Come and lay all your burdens down, for I have more for you than you can see. But you must step up, open your heart and receive!

Here in My presence is where I AM calling you to be. So come, MY daughter, come spend time with ME.

PSALM 32:7 (AMPC)
YOU ARE A HIDING PLACE FOR ME: YOU, LORD, PRESERVE ME FROM TROUBLE. YOU SURROUND ME WITH SONGS AND SHOUTS OF DELIVERANCE. SELAH [PAUSE, AND CALMLY THINK OF THAT]!

The devil is a liar. What's he speaking to you?

_____

What truth, vision or dream has God spoken to you that COMBATS those lies?

_____

_____

LIES OF THE ENEMY

NOT WANTED FEARFUL STUPID
NEVER MEASURE UP LONELINESS
UNFORGIVABLE UGLY

What God says

Eph 1:4, 1 Pet 2:9, John 15:16, Is 43:4, Is 41:10, Is 40:13, 2 Tim 1:7, 1 Cor 2:16, 1 John 2:20, Is 49:2, Jer 29:11, Eph 2:10, Phil 1:6, Phil 4:13, 1 John 4:4, Heb 13:5, Is 43:1, Eph 1:7, 1 John 1:9, Ps 139:14, Is 43:7

What are these scriptures saying to you?

_____

_____

_____

_____

Let Me Show You Off!

Seek first MY kingdom and MY righteousness and watch all things you <u>desire come to be.</u> When you seek ME, oh, how delighted you will be!

Let ME place you center stage. Allow MY glory to penetrate you and surround you and show you off, MY warrior, MY girl, <u>whom I called in this time.</u>

Seek the finer things I say, for you are MY princess, incased with MY light. My favor surrounds you and opens the doors to who you truly are.

You are <u>royalty, precious and pure,</u> a daughter of the KING, mighty and sure.

Allow MY presence to consume you today. Come to that place of worship and lift up your praise.

MY beautiful precious one, come and <u>seek MY face</u> and believe in <u>the one who has called you</u> today <u>out of the darkness</u> and made you <u>brand new</u>.

<u>Come seek MY kingdom.</u> Come here today. Watch all things fall in their place to make you brand new today.

MATHEW 6:33

BUT SEEK FIRST THE KINGDOM OF GOD AND HIS RIGHTEOUSNESS, AND ALL THESE THINGS SHALL BE ADDED TO YOU.

Seek out these great scriptures!

Psalm 37:4, Isaiah 43:1, Isaiah 61:10, 1 Peter 2:9, Psalm 27:8, Colossians 1:13, Matthew 6:33

JUST LISTEN. THEN WRITE!

_____

_____

_____

_____

_____

_____

_____

_____

_____

Whose Battle Is It?

The battle doesn't belong to you but to ME!

I've gone before you. I've made a way. All you need to do is **obey.**

Wait for MY guidance. Wait for ME to say...

"Go forth, go and **pray**!"

Remember it's in MY presence you win. Here you are strengthened from within.

It's MY Spirit that holds you tight. You are surrounded by MY fortress and under MY wings you are safe.

But you first must **believe** and find comfort in MY grace.

So know, MY child, the battles you face all belong to ME. Step aside. Keep moving forward and **finish** your race, knowing the battle is MINE. So relax and find peace.

1 SAMUEL 17:47 (NIV)
ALL THOSE GATHERED HERE WILL KNOW THAT IT IS NOT BY SWORD OR SPEAR THAT THE LORD SAVES;
FOR THE BATTLE IS THE LORD'S, AND HE WILL GIVE ALL OF YOU INTO OUR HANDS."

1 CORINTHIANS 15:57 (AMPC)
BUT THANKS BE TO GOD, WHO GIVES US THE VICTORY [MAKING US CONQUERORS] THROUGH OUR LORD JESUS CHRIST.

NO WEAPON FORMED AGAINST YOU WILL PROSPER. PERIOD.

GOD FIGHTS
GOD PROTECTS
GOD SERVES
GOD LEADS

NO MATTER HOW HARD IT IS.
NO MATTER HOW IT MAY SEEM.
YOU WILL ALWAYS GET THROUGH THE BATTLE.
TRUST HIM. AND YOU WILL SEE.
NEVER GIVE UP!

NO WEAPON FORMED AGAINST YOU WILL PROSPER. PERIOD. ISAIAH 54:17

- -

GOD GIVES GRACE AND PEACE

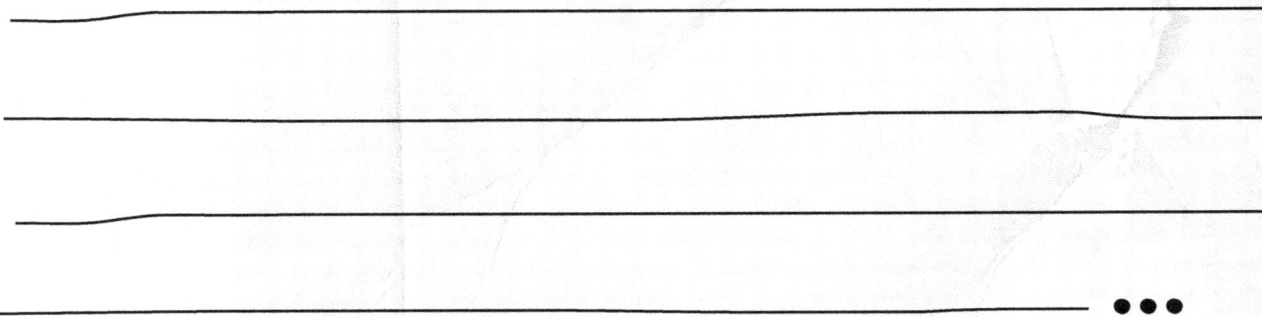

_____

_____

_____

_____ •••

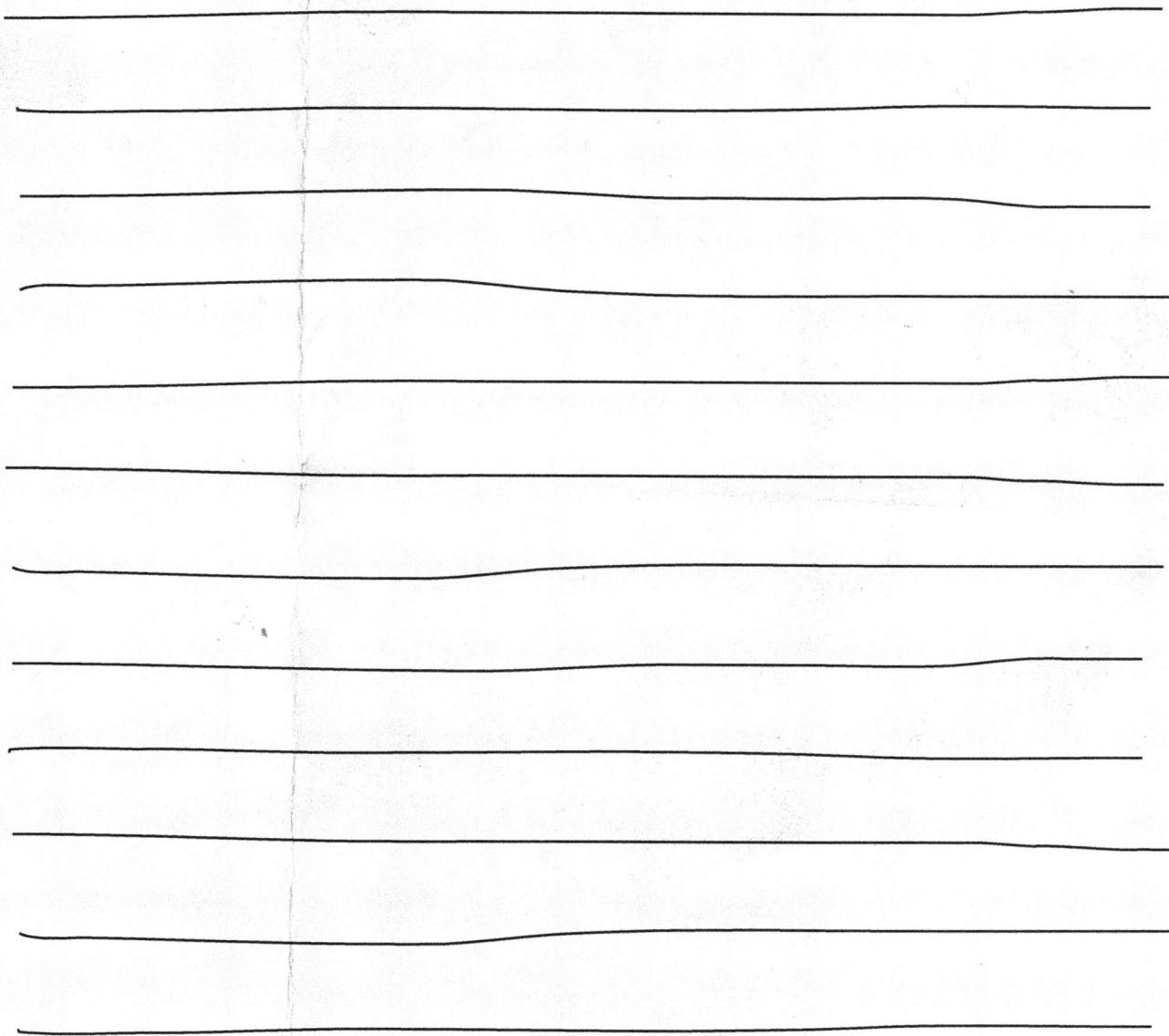

Rise Up

MY dearly beloved, MY daughter, I say: You are MY righteous, MY love and a beauty from within.

You are the one I have called and placed here with ME.

Let go of the rope of despair. Let go of the voices and turn your ear to hear.

I have placed MY hand mighty on you. I have called you out and placed your feet securely on the path of victory.

Don't allow the darkness to draw you in, but hold fast to MY light and hold onto MY word.

It is MY Spirit that will lead you and guide you along, and although you feel discouraged and afraid, you are seeing the dark just before the dawn.

So keep moving forward, MY dear. Keep walking straight along. The path beneath your feet is solid, leading you further, where you belong. MY hand is holding you close, and MY love is deeply penetrating your heart.

 Come close. Come near and hear ME say, "I love you, MY dear. I love who you are. You are MY precious one, the one I adore."

So rise up and know you are MY beloved, the daughter I truly adore.

HEBREWS 10:22-25 (THE MESSAGE)
SO LET'S DO IT FULL OF BELIEF, CONFIDENT THAT WE'RE PRESENTABLE INSIDE AND OUT. LET'S KEEP
A FIRM GRIP ON THE PROMISES THAT KEEP US GOING. HE ALWAYS KEEPS HIS WORD. LET'S SEE HOW INVENTIVE
WE CAN BE IN ENCOURAGING LOVE AND HELPING OUT, NOT AVOIDING WORSHIPING TOGETHER AS
SOME DO BUT SPURRING EACH OTHER ON. ESPECIALLY AS WE SEE THE BIG DAY APPROACHING.

Keep a firm grip on His promises that keep you going. Write out those promises!

_____

_____

_____

_____

_____

_____ •••

You can go anywhere if you're willing to put one foot in front of the other!

Out Of Touch And Not Enough

Sunshine and rain, hot and cold, love and war, peace forever more.

Listen, MY child. Listen to ME. You are more than you can see or even perceive. Although you feel out of touch and not enough, with ME you are overflowing with love, kindness and such.

MY love for you is deeper than you know. As you walk close beside ME daily, remember you're holding tight to MY hand. The demands of this life cannot hold you down.

MY ways are higher, so follow ME. I will take you to the place you need to be.

MY thoughts are above yours, but with ME you will see where it is I have called just you and ME. So don't be downcast and afraid but encouraged and ready to move.

Although you don't see every stone laid in front, believe every step you take is moving you up—up—up!

Come with a smile and joy in your step and follow MY Spirit. You don't need to look right or left.

Trust ME and see. Trust ME and know the steps are leading you places I have planned, ordained, and made for you to go!

It's you and ME in this life; that's all you ever need. Lay it all down now, and just come and follow ME!

PSALM 37:23 (AMPC)
THE STEPS OF A [GOOD] MAN ARE DIRECTED AND ESTABLISHED BY THE LORD WHEN
HE DELIGHTS IN HIS WAY [AND HE BUSIES HIMSELF WITH HIS EVERY STEP].

God loves each of us as if there were only one of us.

ST. AUGUSTINE

Find your favorite psalm.

Pray it out loud.

NOW...WRITE YOUR OWN PSALM.

_____

_____

_____

_____

_____

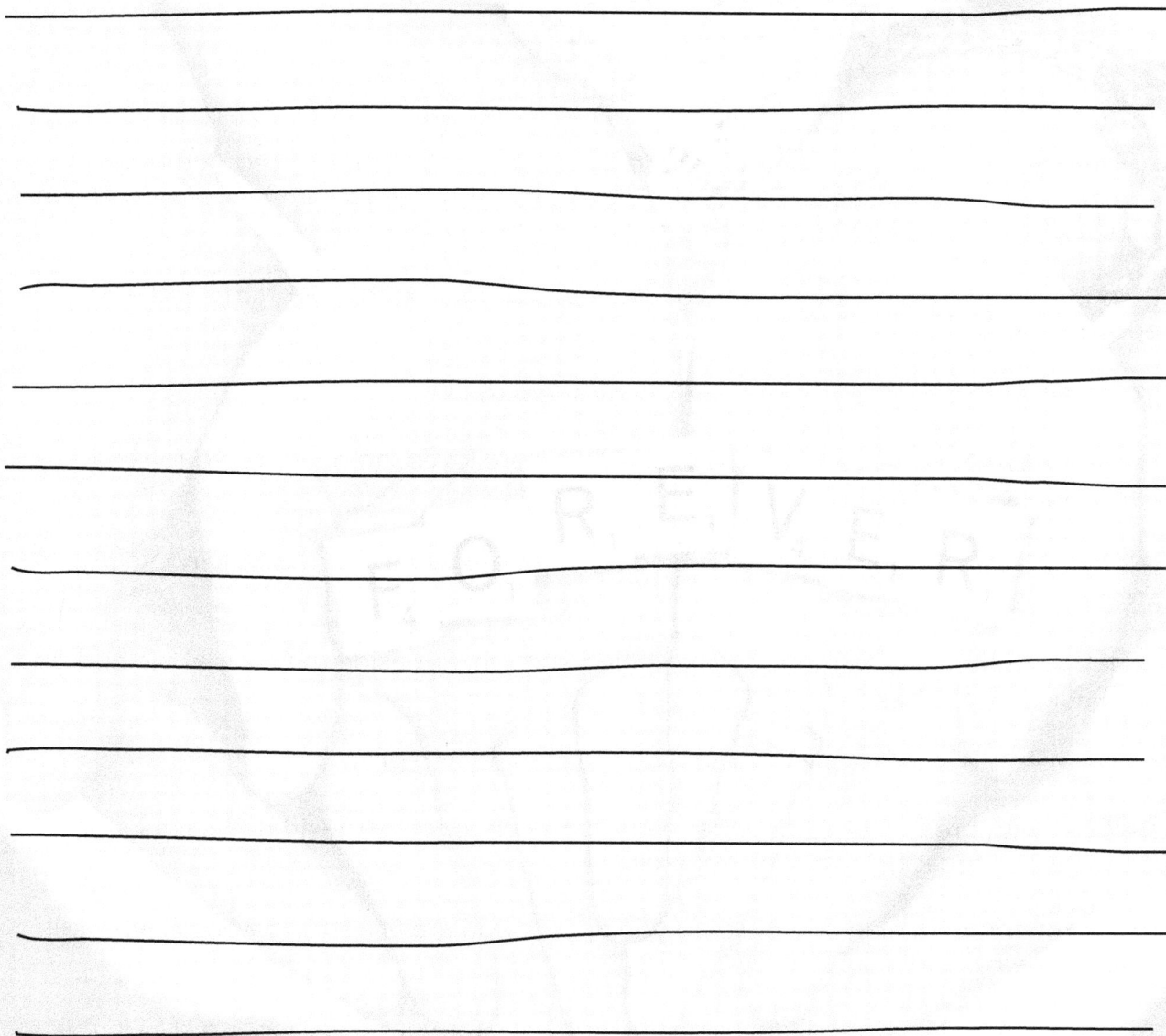

Not Enough, Can't Fit

It is in these times of prayer and in these quiet times that you are filled. Although sometimes you don't see the outcome, believe by faith that the amount of growth, understanding and revelation are going deeper down inside.

Being in MY presence, being close to ME, changes your heart, your hurts and even disappointments.

YOUR HEART says, "I'm not enough, I can't seem to fit."

But **MY HEART** says to you, MY dear one, "YOU are loved, admired, cared for and hand-picked from above."

MY heart beats for you. MY hand is holding you up, and MY Spirit is guiding you strong.

So let go of the past memories of not being enough. Put aside the shame, the hurt and the feeling; it will never change.

It is in MY time and MY chosen path you will expand and grow.

Be filled with great expectation. Be ready to march up onward with MY saints and believe this is a great time to seek MY face.

I AM preparing, training and building you up. For you are MY strong warrior, who will fight battles ahead.

Allow ME to do MY work deep inside and know it's for your own good to stay in this quiet place and dwell.

Listen closely, believe, and be full of great cheer. You are MY daughter, MY own, and you are called for this time and this place.

So expect, wait and believe for the road ahead is mighty indeed!

ISAIAH 40:31 (AMPC)
BUT THOSE WHO WAIT FOR THE LORD [WHO EXPECT, LOOK FOR, AND HOPE IN HIM] SHALL CHANGE AND RENEW THEIR STRENGTH AND POWER; THEY SHALL LIFT THEIR WINGS AND MOUNT UP [CLOSE TO GOD] AS EAGLES [MOUNT UP TO THE SUN]; THEY SHALL RUN AND NOT BE WEARY, THEY SHALL WALK AND NOT FAINT OR BECOME TIRED.

Write these three scriptures out! Declare and confess them *over* yourself!

Romans 8:37 (AMPC) – I am more than a conqueror in Christ!

_____

_____

Ephesians 1:4 (AMPC) – I am chosen and hand-picked by Jesus!

_____

_____

Philippians 4:13 (AMPC) – I can do all things through Jesus Christ!

_____

_____

Those Voices

In MY presence your heart is healed, your mind is calm and your emotions laid to rest.

Come child, come quietly in MY presence and lay everything down.
Talk if you'd like. Cry, scream or just be still.

It's okay. Just come and allow ME to comfort you, love you, and pour MYSELF all over you.

You allow life's issues to overwhelm you. You hear voices of inadequacy, unworthiness and lack.

But in MY presence you see things differently. You are able to hush the voices. You're able to sit still and hear ME say...

You are loved. You are worthy. You are a child of the Most High God, and you are called and chosen for a great purpose.

I have great plans for your future. I have all MY storehouses full, but you must come and allow ME to fill you full.

Come this day, and spend time with ME and enjoy this special time.

I promise you it will not go unrewarded, and you will leave full, refreshed and made new.

Come into MY presence...Come!

JEREMIAH 29:11 (NIV)
FOR I KNOW THE PLANS I HAVE FOR YOU," DECLARES THE LORD. "PLANS TO PROSPER
YOU AND NOT TO HARM YOU. PLANS TO GIVE YOU HOPE AND A FUTURE.

2 THESSALONIANS 2:13-14 (THE MESSAGE)

MEANWHILE, WE'VE GOT OUR HANDS FULL CONTINUALLY THANKING GOD FOR YOU, OUR GOOD FRIENDS—SO LOVED BY GOD! GOD PICKED YOU OUT AS HIS FROM THE VERY START. THINK OF IT: INCLUDED IN GOD'S ORIGINAL PLAN OF SALVATION BY THE BOND OF FAITH IN THE LIVING TRUTH. THIS IS THE LIFE OF THE SPIRIT HE INVITED YOU TO THROUGH THE MESSAGE WE DELIVERED, IN WHICH YOU GET IN ON THE GLORY OF OUR MASTER, JESUS CHRIST.

You don't have to be invited into God's throne room. Just come boldly to the throne of grace (Hebrews 4:16).

COME INTO MY PRESENCE! LET MY LOVE OVERWHELM YOU!

WRITE IT. DECLARE IT. DO IT.
AND ENJOY HIS PRESENCE.

_____

_____

_____

_____

_____

_____

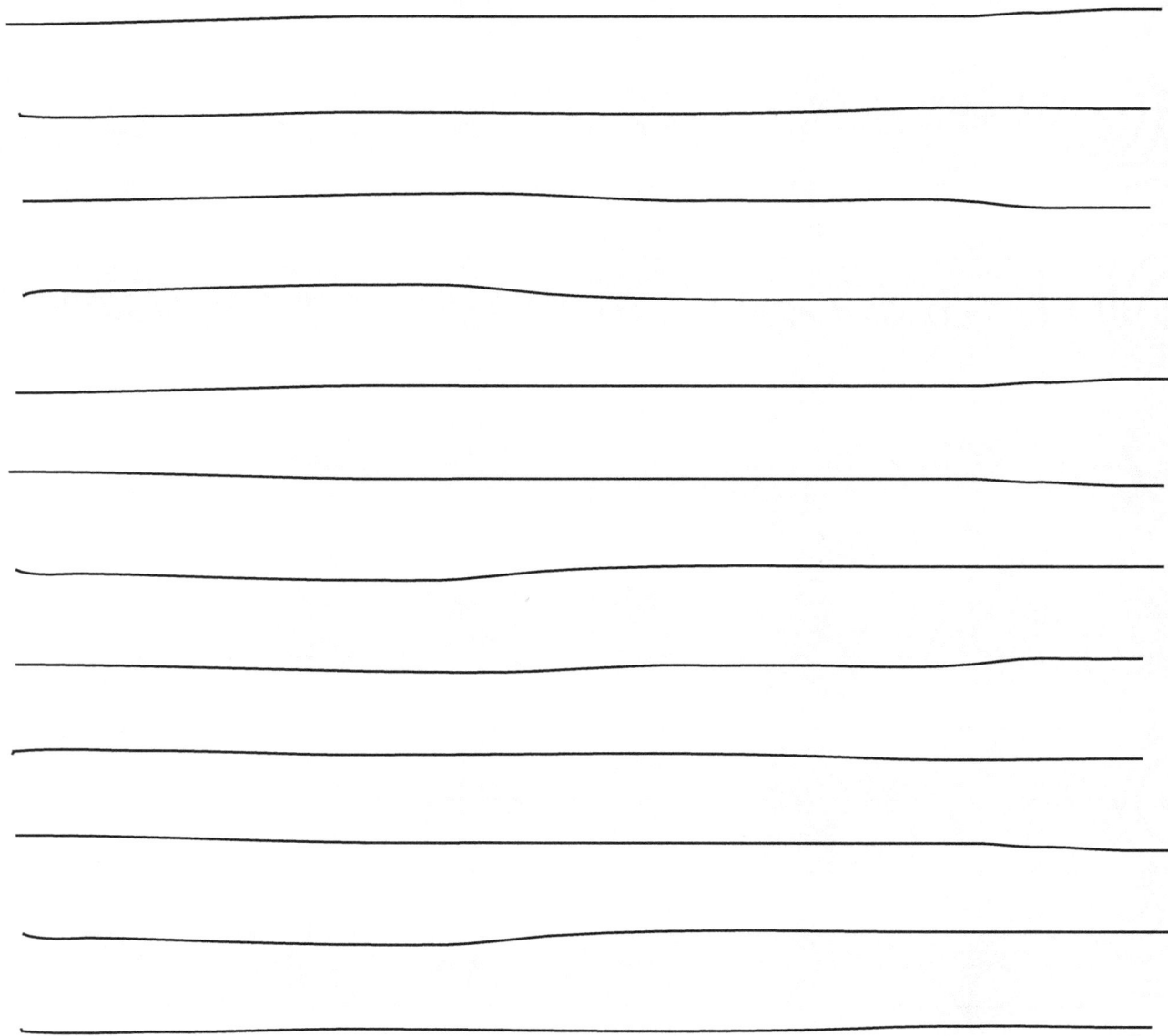

_____

_____

_____

_____

_____

_____

_____

_____

HIS LOVE IS DEEP. HIS LOVE IS WIDE AND IT COVERS US. HIS LOVE IS FIERCE. HIS LOVE IS STRONG, IT IS FURIOUS. HIS LOVE IS SWEET. HIS LOVE IS WILD AND IT'S WAKING HEARTS TO LIFE.

Furious
Jeremy Riddle

What's Your Name?

Before the earth was formed, I **picked** you to be MINE.

Before you knew your name, I called you **holy, blameless** and **pure**.

It is I who have **called you by name**. It is I who have said, "Yes! That's the one I choose!"

So don't compare yourself, MY dear. Don't look at others in envy and want to be someone else.

No, you are **one-of-a-kind, hand-picked, chosen** and **called** for MY purpose on this earth.

MY purpose is to touch the hearts and souls of those I have placed along your way.

So believe with a heart open and ready to go, ready to receive and ready to pour out love on those hurting and crying out for ME.

Hand-picked you are, **chosen** and **called** only for ME.

Wow! What a mighty call and privilege it is to be a part of the heavenly host.

You are **redeemed, sanctified** and the **righteousness** of ME, **clothed** in white linens and decked out in **jewels**.

Oh, MY **beautiful** daughter. Stay in this place so close to ME that all you see and all you believe is who **you truly are in ME**.

Step into that place. Step in and believe.

ISAIAH 61:10 (AMPC)

I WILL GREATLY REJOICE IN THE LORD, MY SOUL WILL EXULT IN MY GOD; FOR HE HAS CLOTHED ME WITH THE GARMENTS OF SALVATION. HE HAS COVERED ME WITH THE ROBE OF RIGHTEOUSNESS, AS A BRIDEGROOM DECKS HIMSELF WITH A GARLAND, AND AS A BRIDE ADORNS HERSELF WITH HER JEWELS.

We all have a name our parents gave us, but do you know God has a special name for you, too?

Ask Him!

Be still and listen! — REVELATION 2:17

_____

_____

_____

_____

_____

_____

_____

Be Proud

Seek ME and find ME when you seek ME with all your heart. I AM always waiting and listening to all your wants and all your fears!

Come to MY throne. Come in and stay. Lay everything down.

MY love will overtake you. MY glory is all around. Just come in, MY dear, and pick up your glorious crown, place it on your head and walk away proud.

Be proud of who you are and where I've planted you to be. It's a time of reflection and time to look around. See the mighty changes, the Spirit within. HE has called you up. HE is drawing you in.

So seek ME, MY child. Seek ME today, and when you find ME, believe it's going to be a great and mighty day!

JEREMIAH 29:13
... AND YOU WILL SEEK ME AND FIND ME, WHEN YOU SEARCH FOR ME WITH ALL YOUR HEART.

HEBREWS 4:16 (AMPC)
LET US THEN FEARLESSLY AND CONFIDENTLY AND BOLDLY DRAW NEAR TO THE THRONE OF GRACE (THE THRONE OF GOD'S UNMERITED FAVOR TO US SINNERS), THAT WE MAY RECEIVE MERCY [FOR OUR FAILURES] AND FIND GRACE TO HELP IN GOOD TIME FOR EVERY NEED [APPROPRIATE HELP AND WELL-TIMED HELP, COMING JUST WHEN WE NEED IT].

How cool is it that God is actually proud of you!?

You should be, too!

WRITE DOWN THINGS YOU'RE PROUD OF, AND GIVE GOD THE GLORY!

_____

_____

_____

_____

_____

_____

_____

_____

_____

U Will Shine

Glory and splendor, majesty I AM. The king of glory, the Spirit from within. Wrapped in light, for all the world to see. Holy, Almighty, I AM the King of Kings!

Hold tight, MY dear. Hold on with all your might and believe the Savior has said, "Come! Come into the light! Let ME clean you up and wash your sins away. Then you can walk out clean and ready for the day!"

Know you are shining bright, shining bright for ME today. Showing MY glory, MY majesty and all that I have to say.

So allow MY Spirit to change you and become the woman I have said. You will shine for ME today. Go forth and know MY glory, MY splendor. The Lord of Hosts has called you and picked you out for HIMSELF.

Come, MY daughter! Come and grab hold of MY mighty and glorious hand. Walk with ME. Talk with ME and glean all you can. Know the Savior of the world has placed you strong and secure on solid ground.

You are moving forward, fearless, courageous and mighty in the land.

Glorious splendor, that is all I AM.

PSALM 104:1-2 (NIV)
PRAISE THE LORD, MY SOUL. LORD MY GOD, YOU ARE VERY GREAT;
YOU ARE CLOTHED WITH SPLENDOR AND MAJESTY. THE LORD WRAPS HIMSELF IN LIGHT
AS WITH A GARMENT; HE STRETCHES OUT THE HEAVENS LIKE A TENT

MATTHEW 5:16 (AMPC)
LET YOUR LIGHT SO SHINE BEFORE MEN THAT THEY MAY SEE YOUR MORAL EXCELLENCE AND YOUR PRAISEWORTHY, NOBLE, AND GOOD DEEDS AND RECOGNIZE AND HONOR AND PRAISE AND GLORIFY YOUR FATHER WHO IS IN HEAVEN.

GLORY | HONOR | POWER

GLORY, GLORY, THAT IS WHO YOU ARE! GLORIOUS, MIGHTY, MY REDEEMER WHO KNEW ME FROM THE START!

GLORY, GLORY, YOU ARE MY GOD, MIGHTY, STRONG AND TRUE.
GLORY, GLORY, THAT IS WHO YOU ARE, MY GOD THROUGH AND THROUGH!

Your turn! You write out your song, poem or prayer to Him!

_____

_____

_____

_____

_____

_____

Put Away The Toys

No more lies. No more fairy tales. But open your heart up and hear the truth be told. Listen to the voice of the Spirit and let HIM be your guide. There is no other way than to follow MY lead. There is no other path but the one beneath your feet.

Child, hear ME say, "Step up. Step up and hear the trumpet sound. Listen to the mighty horn and listen to it well. It is a time to go deeper, deeper than before; so put away the trinkets and all the noisy toys."

Come before ME. Come and rest yourself. For the road beneath your feet is taking you up to places for you to dwell. Look beyond this world to see spiritual things, to open up your eyes to see what I see. Look beneath the surface, look beyond despair and see the hearts open and ready for repair.

So come, MY child, put all childish things aside. Walk close beside ME. We are moving quickly. We're moving in MY time.

1 CORINTHIANS 13:11 (AMP)
WHEN I WAS A CHILD, I TALKED LIKE A CHILD, I THOUGHT LIKE A CHILD, I REASONED LIKE A CHILD;
NOW THAT I HAVE BECOME A MAN, I AM DONE WITH CHILDISH WAYS AND HAVE PUT THEM ASIDE.

It's time to put away the toys and distractions. Put away something that's important to you today! Instead, spend your time seeking the deeper things of God.

What happened?

_____

_____

_____

_____

_____

_____

_____

MAKE THIS A HABIT!

A Father to the Fatherless

I **AM** clothed in glory and full of power.

I **AM** strong, mighty and know all things.

I **AM** the same yesterday, today and forever, and I do not lie.

I **AM** the GOD ALMIGHTY, sovereign and good. I looked from heaven and said, "Yes! It's very good."

I **AM** the FATHER to the fatherless. I **AM** THE KING OF KINGS.

I AM the GOD who loves and gives generously.

It is I who have called you. It is I who have said, "Yes, you are MINE." So child, hear ME when I speak to you. You are MY daughter, a mighty soldier for the Lord. You are redeemed, forgiven and made in the image of ME.

Come to ME, come and stay awhile, and let ME build you up firm, steady and strong. I AM calling you up. I AM saying to you that this is the generation I have chosen for you. It is in this time you will go forth and change the nation with MY words.

So prepare yourself in ME and lay your burdens down. Choose to follow ME and wear your mighty crown. It's time. It's time to step in and know the hand of the Almighty has placed you here.

I **AM** GOD. I **AM** HE. I **AM** THE ONE who will never leave.

Come and follow ME, and boy, will you see! GOD ALMIGHTY, the GOD who always sees. GOD ALMIGHTY, that is who I **AM**. Come, child, and lay it all down.

PSALM 68:5
A FATHER OF THE FATHERLESS, A DEFENDER OF WIDOWS, IS GOD IN HIS HOLY HABITATION.

HEBREW 13:8
JESUS CHRIST IS THE SAME YESTERDAY, TODAY, AND FOREVER.

No matter how good or bad your natural father is, your heavenly Father lavishes His love all over you.

Look up three scriptures that tell you how much He loves you—and what it means to you!

_____

_____

_____

_____

_____

_____

Write a letter to your natural father. Pour out your heart, hurts and desires. Then forgive him. Rip it up and throw it away.

_____

_____

_____

_____

_____

_____

_____

_____

_____

_____

Don't Throw Your Hands In The Air!

Cruel, unkind and dark. Unclean and hard.
Sitting alone hearing voices all around, believing the lies and giving myself out.
Sickness, disease, death all around. What is left if I lay it all down?
All my heart says is, "What else is there? How can this be? Is this all there is?
If God is full of love, as they say, why do I see pain every day?
Why does HE allow all this? Why doesn't HE stop all the sickness?"

People are hurting, crying out for ME, but without the help of MY loved ones no one can see.

No man can know the love I have if no one will step up and say, "Yes I can!"

Don't throw your hands up in the air. Don't look away from all the despair but put your trust in ME. Come open your heart and follow ME.

Although the darkness is thick, MY love can penetrate deep and change the atmosphere.

Yes, you are correct. I AM a God who loves even the sick. I'M a God who died for you all.

I AM the one who has chosen you for this call.

It's a new time and a new sound. So keep your eyes open and your heart on alert and wait for the call of MY trumpet to sound.

Hear MY heartbeat like a heavy drum and stand tall in the gap for those ready to fall.

Come, MY child, come with ME. Don't look at the circumstances, look only to ME.

It's not at all what you think. So remember I AM the God who will defeat!
I AM the one who will win it all.

Cast aside every burden and care. Come boldly with your hands raised in the air, ready to receive power from on high.

And go forth in this place and show off MY light to let MY love shine ... **Jesus Christ.**

1 PETER 5:7
CASTING THE WHOLE OF YOUR CARE [ALL YOUR ANXIETIES, ALL YOUR WORRIES, ALL YOUR CONCERNS, ONCE AND FOR ALL] ON HIM, FOR HE CARES FOR YOU AFFECTIONATELY AND CARES ABOUT YOU WATCHFULLY.

EPHESIANS 4:17-19 (THE MESSAGE)
AND SO I INSIST—AND GOD BACKS ME UP ON THIS—THAT THERE BE NO GOING ALONG WITH THE CROWD, THE EMPTY-HEADED, MINDLESS CROWD. THEY'VE REFUSED FOR SO LONG TO DEAL WITH GOD THAT THEY'VE LOST TOUCH NOT ONLY WITH GOD BUT WITH REALITY ITSELF. THEY CAN'T THINK STRAIGHT ANYMORE. FEELING NO PAIN, THEY LET THEMSELVES GO IN SEXUAL OBSESSION, ADDICTED TO EVERY SORT OF PERVERSION.

How can you be different today? Pick which one you'll do today!

- Pray for someone
- Encourage someone
- Give help to a homeless person
- Show love to someone

Enough Already

If your heart is full of things of this world, how can MY LOVE penetrate you?

When you look to the dark to fill you up, how will you notice the light shining brightly, deep within your heart?

Child, you fear and you fret! You feel overwhelmed and out of sorts because you look for reassurance deep in the dark.

MY LOVE is always radiating for you. MY embrace is here with arms opened wide; but if you turn away, run and hide, you can get caught up in the ways of this world. It will only disappoint you and make you feel like a fool.

Believe MY ways are true. MY path will lead you to wholeness and new life.

Why be downcast and afraid when MY Spirit is leading and guiding your way?

You are powerful, redeemed and MINE. You can do all things with ME living on the inside. You are hand-chosen, with a mighty call. Redeemed from all sin, cleaned up and made whole!

So come now, MY daughter, let's take a new path just you and ME, away from all the darkness. Shine and walk in a new light, full of glory and with a new name.

Holy, pure and mighty you are! One-of-a-kind, redeemed, a mighty warrior for the Lord your God!

PSALM 119:105
YOUR WORD IS A LAMP TO MY FEET AND A LIGHT TO MY PATH.

1 JOHN 2:15
DO NOT LOVE THE WORLD OR THE THINGS IN THE WORLD. IF ANYONE LOVES THE WORLD, THE LOVE OF THE FATHER IS NOT IN HIM.

Have you ever wanted something or to do something not pleasing to God? Did you find out it's not as fun as you thought or as it used to be? Did you find disappointment in it? Write it out!

Now...ask God to reveal a new path to you!

_____

_____

_____

_____

_____

He Is Coming

Come and see! Come and see!

The great and mighty ONE, coming in the clouds for everyone.

Oh, HIS glory, HIS mighty majesty! Bow your knee and delight yourself with glee.

The SAVIOR, the KING OF KINGS and all HIS heavenly hosts. Oh, marvelous, marvelous to most is HE.

Striking and powerful fire that burns. HE is returning soon for those HE has called.

So come, MY child. Come as fast as you can. Be ready, for the King is coming to grab hold of your hand.

REVELATION 22:12
...'AND BEHOLD, I AM COMING QUICKLY, AND MY REWARD IS WITH ME,
TO GIVE TO EVERY ONE ACCORDING TO HIS WORK.

MARK 13:26 (NLT)
THEN EVERYONE WILL SEE THE SON OF MAN COMING ON THE CLOUDS WITH GREAT POWER AND GLORY.

JESUS IS COMING!

R U READY?

How can u ready someone else?

_____

_____

_____

_____

_____

_____

_____

My life is no longer my own

Although my life is not at all what I thought, I continue to grow in the things of God.

Although I still hurt and sometimes fall apart, I will continue to follow the plans God has placed deep in my heart.

And though the steps are not always seen, I know HE guides me and takes me beyond the walls surrounding me, with HIS marvelous light pulling me along.

I've learned to trust wholly in HIM and not lean on my own insight but follow the Spirit from within.

Today I say. Today I declare, God is my light, my confidante, my strength. I know HE is always here, saying, "Come on, MY child, come on with ME, for I have the plans written out clearly."

So here I come, stepping out boldly, stepping up proclaiming HIS kingdom come. I say proudly to my God, "Here I am. Do as YOU will, for my life is no longer my own. YOUR will be done.

Write your own poem to Him!

_____

_____

_____

_____

_____

_____

_____

_____

_____

_____

The Doorway to Radical Love

Meeting Jesus Christ as your Lord and Savior is the doorway to you feeling radically loved and loving radically.

Praying this prayer is quick and easy, and it's the best decision you'll ever make. Simply pray these words from your heart aloud.

Father, in the name of Jesus, I come to you today to receive Jesus as my Lord and Savior. Your Word says if I confess with my mouth and believe with my heart that Jesus died and was raised from the dead, I will be saved. Your Word also says if we confess our sins, You are faithful and just to forgive us of all unrighteousness.

So, today I receive You into my heart. I make You the Lord of my life. I surrender to YOUR will.

Because of You

I am the righteousness of God through Christ.

I am forgiven.

I am more than conqueror in Christ Jesus.

I am worthy, holy, pure and blameless before You.

I have the same Spirit in me as Jesus has in Him, and I have all the authority He has given me in the name of Jesus.

In the eyes of the Savior, you're radically, deeply and lavishly loved!

Almighty God has called you, chosen you and spoken in your life that you're to be lifted high and above.

Believe and know you are hand-picked, redeemed and made to go places to change the world.

You're not here by chance or by accident or made to fall away from His love. You're here for a purpose and a reason only He and you know.

Through this journey of love, know and take courage that your life is now no longer stuck, but your feet have been planted firmly and your heart is fit tightly like a glove.

Be strong, courageous and believe you will and can overcome anything.

You will achieve much more than you can see, when you place all your trust in Him and let your heart be transformed and full of all of God's love.

Remember who you are, and when things get dark, remember you are a child of the Most High God!

LET'S END THIS with a Bang!

Lamb of God
EL SHADDIAH
God of miracles
Everlasting love
lover of my soul
Just true
Full of glory
Signs and wonders

You are God
All-knowing
Precious
Redeemer
TRUE
Last
First
Mighty
Powerful
Truthful
Majestic
Glorious
HOLY
FULL OF POWER
LOVING FAITHFUL
PROTECTOR
Victorious

END FROM THE BEGINNING
Great I AM
ALMIGHTY

YOU KNOW EVERY HAIR ON MY HEAD
Jehovah Jireh
MY KING

YOU ARE MY HEALER, SAVIOR, FRIEND
My provider
ALPHA AND OMEGA

Yahweh
MY SHIELD
My banner
LION OF JUDAH

BELOVED
YOU ARE EVERYTHING
JEHOVAH NISSI
GOD WHO SEES
COMPASSIONATE

About the Author

Monica Withers is a woman with a mission. She's passionate about sharing with women everywhere how much God loves them and desires a deeply personal relationship with each of us.

As a personal trainer and instructor for 30 years, Monica devoted her professional life to empowering women to shape their bodies. Yet, ultimately, Monica realized it's even more rewarding to empower women to know their Creator as Father God and fellowship with Him on a daily basis. Founder of Radical God, second-time author and Bible school graduate, Monica travels sharing how God's love transformed her life and will do the same for you.

In groups large and small, Monica often shares with young women how she experienced firsthand the grip and snare of the enemy and lived in the despair, deception and insecurity it brings. But those dark days were long ago replaced with a fiery passion to teach women how to rise up in the power and authority of Jesus Christ and live a life of freedom, love, security and joy almost beyond belief.

Monica has been married to her best friend and partner, Mark, for 33 years. They make their home in Tulsa, Oklahoma. For more information about the God Talk series, new releases, the Radical God product line of clothes, jewelry and more, check out **www.radicalgod.com**.

MONICA WITHERS

monica@radicalgod.com

www.radicalgod.com

f MONICA WITHERS

RADICALGODTALK

571.527.8348

www.ingramcontent.com/pod-product-compliance
Lightning Source LLC
Chambersburg PA
CBHW081229090426
42738CB00016B/3229

Patricia Taylor Wells published her first book in 2016: "Camp Tyler, A First of its Kind" for the benefit of Camp Tyler, the oldest outdoor education school in the country, which she attended as a child. Since then, Ms. Wells has published the following books: *The Eyes of the Doe*, 2017 (novel), *Mademoiselle Renoir à Paris*, 2018 (memoir), *LodeStar: Reflections of Light and Dark*, 2019 (poetry), *The Sand Rose*, 2021 (novel), and *Kaleidoscope*, 2022 (poetry). Her awards include First Place for Family Life/Inspirational Fiction in the Best of Texas Book Awards in 2018 (*The Eyes of the Doe*), First Place for Poetry in the Best of Texas Book Awards in 2020 (*LodeStar: Reflections of Light and Dark*), and First Place for Poetry in the Indie Authors Awards in 2023 (*Kaleidoscope*). Since 2019, she has also received ten awards for short stories. Since 2016, *Tyler Today Magazine* has featured Ms. Wells seven times in its "Authors Among Us" column, which she helped inspire to benefit local authors. Ms. Wells, who holds a BA in English and French, facilitated writing critique groups for the Atlanta Writers Club and Knoxville Writers Group. She especially enjoys writing poetry and draws inspiration from the wide range of experiences she gathered from her travels and living in various places.

Please visit her website at **www.patricia-taylor-wells.com**

www.ingramcontent.com/pod-product-compliance
Lightning Source LLC
LaVergne TN
LVHW061336060426
835511LV00014B/1944